Green Design

A Healthy Home Handbook

Green Design

A Healthy Home Handbook

Alan Berman

FRANCES LINCOLN LIMITED
PUBLISHERS

DEBT OF GRATITUDE

A small number of prescient individuals began, some 30 years ago, to talk about new ways of living and to design solutions to problems that the rest of the world at the time didn't even know existed. Out on the fringe and ahead of their time, these ideas are today central to our future. Beside the groundbreaking work of those people, this book pales into insignificance. The list is long but those I can readily identify are: Christopher Alexander, Wendell Berry, Rachel Carson, Paul Ekins, Paul Ehrlich, Paul Hawken, Ivan Illich, Amory Lovins, Bill McKibben, D. Meadows, Victor Papanak, David Pearson, Sim Van Der Ryn, Fritz Schumacher, John Seymour, John Todd, and Robert and Brenda Vale. Also deserving mention are the visionaries who started, among many organizations, The Sierra Club, Friends of the Earth, Greenpeace and the Centre for Alternative Technology. To these and many other eco-thinkers, the world owes an incalculable debt. Their achievement will be properly celebrated when the rest of us start putting in place the actions they have so long advocated.

PLEASE NOTE

Photographs do not purport to show interiors that are entirely safe but to illustrate some of the issues discussed that give existing buildings a greater degree of safety.

This book is not intended to replace specialist medical advice. The author makes no claim to medical expertise. Arguments propounded are based on a broad consensus of views from the sources listed and refer to the generality of materials and processes. In some cases the particulars of individual products might differ from the views expressed.

Frances Lincoln Limited
4 Torriano Mews, Torriano Avenue
London NW5 2RZ
www.franceslincoln.com

Green Design
Copyright © Frances Lincoln Limited 2001, 2008
Text copyright © Alan Berman 2001, 2008
Photographs credited on page 192

First Frances Lincoln Edition
(as *Healthy Home Handbook*): 2001
Revised edition: 2008

British Library Cataloguing-in-Publication Data
A catalogue record for this book is available from the British Library

ISBN 978-0-7112-2834-4

Printed in Singapore

9 8 7 6 5 4 3 2 1

INTRODUCTION

NATURAL SOURCES
Locally made bricks and local timber used as boards and logs are from natural, safe and renewable sources (above and above right).

HOME-MAKING IS A CREATIVE ACT. It involves design decisions and choices which have always been guided by three principles: everything had to be practical, robust and beautiful. The Romans called these principles 'commodity', 'firmness' and 'delight'. Today a fourth factor must be taken into account – safety. All design needs to be safe, both for our health and that of the planet. This book aims to show that it is possible to create homes that are safe as well as being attractive.

Before the advent in the nineteenth century of industries driven by fossil fuel, people made things in ways that by and large followed the biological patterns of nature and were safe. Resources used were naturally renewable, had few harmful side effects and degraded safely when obsolete. Low demand meant that any damage to the earth was small and in time was generally repaired through natural processes. But today, the earth can no longer sustain the demands placed upon it. Progress and growth is driven by ever-increasing consumption, which generates increasing volumes of waste. Dirty factories powered by fossil fuels produce, on average, 28 kilograms of waste for each kilogram of useful product they manufacture. We usually replace today's objects with tomorrow's, not because they have worn out, but because their appearance has become unfashionable – most consumer products become waste after about six weeks.

The first edition of this book was written seven years ago when many people were aware of climate change, but governments and most decision makers were in denial. Since then, even the most sceptical have recognised what is happening. Unpredictable and extreme weather conditions world wide have now, literally, entered everyone's home. When we can no longer insure low-lying homes against storm and flood, when children can no longer safely sunbathe or swim in rivers, when friends are lost to natural disasters such as the 2005 tsunami, it is clear that the once finely tuned relationship between humankind and nature is out of balance. We have arrived at a point of diminishing returns – the more we produce and consume, the more we destroy the capacity of the world to provide these improvements. The need for immediate action is critical: climatologists advise that we are near the point beyond which the world's eco-system will not repair itself. Fortunately, acknowledgment of the problem has led to a huge increase in the availability of information and products so that we can now make and run our homes

WOOD
The boarded walls of these New England houses are in harmony with the surrounding woods, from which materials have been culled.

LOCAL MATERIALS

These homes look right in their settings. The sturdy walls of the rural French houses (below right) have been built with stone found on the site. The rich reddish-brown of these terracotta roofs in a Mediterranean village (below left) is the colour of the local earth from which the tiles are made. Wood and cedar shingles from nearby forests was used for the sun-bleached decking and wall cladding on this luxurious ocean-front veranda (bottom).

to ensure a much reduced impact on the global environment. Most notably, understanding the importance of reducing domestic energy consumption has led to new energy-efficient systems for the home: the pros and cons of the many different systems are reviewed in the last chapter.

The destruction of global health is mirrored by a similar impact on our personal health. Tens of thousands of chemicals in use today in the home and elsewhere are known to be toxic. The alarming growth of twentieth-century diseases – the increase in child asthma, for example – should at least cause us to wonder about the link between the chemicals that surround us and our health.

SIMPLE, BASIC MATERIALS
Simple materials such as grasses and bamboo provide rich texture in homes (above). New uses for basic materials challenge designers' ingenuity – this chair is made from recycled cardboard (above right).

Ultimately, living in harmony with the earth requires that all homes are constructed with materials that are sustainable, so as to consume as little energy as possible and be safe. But most people cannot change the way in which their homes are constructed, and can only aim to make them as comfortable and safe as possible. The choice and quantities of materials used in home decorating make a huge contribution to the safety and health of both planet and home, and this book aims to outline a number of design strategies to help make homes that are satisfying, while minimizing their impact on the global environment and on our health.

REINTERPRETING VERNACULAR DESIGN

First, we can develop an approach to design that is based on the way in which vernacular builders have for ages built and decorated homes. Pre-industrial homes used local natural materials sparingly, functionally and elegantly to make homes that were in tune with their local physical and climatic context. One rule of vernacular production recurs regularly in contemporary design – the idea of achieving more by using less. The most pleasing homes are often those in which economy and elegance of design create satisfying objects and maximize the enjoyment of space, light and sunshine, together with the texture, colour and form of materials. Different materials and elements in the home are examined, and the lessons of vernacular cultures reinterpreted for today, in chapter one.

NATURE'S CYCLES
Trees grow by means of energy from the sun and nourishment from compost in the soil extracted by their root system.

Another strategy for sustainability is to use passive, low-energy techniques for making comfortable homes. Local materials and devices tuned to local climates have always done this – techniques that we have forgotten since comfort became available at the flick of a switch. Ways in which we can do this are discussed in chapter two.

Further exciting opportunities for sustainability lie in the beginnings of a revolution that replaces materials made using dirty, wasteful methods with those resulting from clean processes. Manufacturing processes are being modelled on nature's cyclical patterns. Clean production can make objects that will biodegrade and become resources for the next benign cycle, thereby minimizing resource depletion and polluting wastes. Manufacturers in the USA and Germany in particular are demonstrating that such sustainable processes not only work but are economically viable. Safe materials and techniques, old and new, are explored in chapter three.

Many of the issues discussed in this book relate to risk. Just because we cannot see the dangerous effects of modern chemicals and electromagnetic radiation, for example, does not mean they do not exist. Nor can we rely on producers to provide us only with products that are safe, when doing so may reduce their profits. Today we are exposed to risks never before experienced. The body may be likened to a vessel that has evolved to hold a certain amount of toxic stress. But the risk is that at a certain point – and everyone's threshold will be different – it will hold no more and will overflow into illness.

Our buying and furnishing habits have worldwide effects on labour conditions and social and ethical issues, no less than on the environment. These must be taken into account, and while we cannot always know what happens in faraway countries, there are organizations that do. Buying 'fair trade' products helps to encourage and support ethical production practices.

Many of the demands for a sustainable home conflict with each other and with ethical issues. Responsible design needs to take into account the issues involved in design choice – personal circumstances, global and personal environmental health, transport issues as well as ethical production. This book offers no simple answers and prescribes no particular design or style, but aims to lay out the more significant of these aspects, so as to allow you to establish your own priorities for choice. Homes that are lastingly satisfying start a virtuous circle: there will be little reason to change them simply to follow fashion, thereby reducing resource depletion and wasteful consumption. If this book helps to create just a few safe and sustainable homes with less of an impact on the health of the earth, then it will have been worthwhile.

Chapter One

DESIGN AND ENVIRONMENT

NO HOME IS AN ISLAND

THE CHOICE OF ANY ITEM FOR THE HOME, such as a chair, floor covering or paint, may seem a straightforward matter. But dig a little deeper into the origins of that item and a vast web of global and personal health issues is revealed. At every stage, from the raw materials used, to manufacture and transport and through its useful life until it is discarded, every household item has an impact on our environment – and thus on our lives.

The global environmental crisis stems from the fact that while nature works with benign and productive life cycles, industrial processes are usually destructive. Nature's cycles are like a closed loop – biological processes, fuelled by the sun, make materials that grow and have a useful life until they bio-degrade, becoming a resource from which new materials can grow. In contrast, many first-generation industrial processes are linear: they take resources, use energy to process them, and make products with a short lifespan and by-products that become useless, often poisonous, waste.

Every household item has an impact on our environment and our lives

Two simple chairs, both classics of design – a traditional ladderback chair with solid wood legs, seat and back, and a chair with a moulded plywood seat and back and chrome-plated steel legs – illustrate these differences. The wooden ladderback chair, which might be anything from a simple, rough-hewn example to the elegant version created by the Shakers in eighteenth-century New England, was made from wood grown in local forests, which regenerate themselves naturally. The timber was taken to workshops nearby (sometimes in the forest itself) and the chair was made using simple tools that consumed a minimum amount of energy. The beeswax finish and any glues needed were local, animal-based products. Employment of craftsmen living nearby sustained the local economy as well as the woodland. Any wood waste was used to make smaller items and fuel, or in animal bedding. If the chair broke, it could – and still can – be repaired, using simple skills. When it was finally disposed of, the whole chair would rot to produce safe and regenerative organic matter – an example of a closed loop, a benign life cycle that does very little damage to the environment.

The plywood and steel chair, on the other hand, has a negative impact on the environment. The steel for the legs contains iron ore – a finite resource that requires energy to mine, transport and refine. More energy is used to transport the ore to a factory, where it is made into steel tube. This is transported to a stockholder, who sends it on again to be formed into legs, which are sent away for chroming – a high-energy process that produces toxic waste. Meanwhile, in another part of the world, trees are felled for the plywood seat. The wood is transported to huge machines for slicing into thin veneers; these are laminated together under heat and pressure, using dangerous chemical glues to bond the sheets into plywood. The plywood is taken to another factory where it is moulded into the seat and back – again under considerable heat. Here they are coated with a range of polyurethanes, PVCs and solvent coatings. When the plywood and steel parts finally meet, the result is a chair that is almost impossible to repair – although some steel may be recycled. When its relatively short useful life is over, the chair ends up in a landfill site and leaches pollution into the ground as the chemical glues and chrome degrade.

THE RIGHT CHOICES

Most of the items used to furnish and decorate our homes undergo a wide range of processes in their manufacture, including colouring, dyeing, printing, treating and washing,

as well as that huge waste generator – packaging. Our two chairs demonstrate the essential principles that link design choices to the global environment: the consumption of natural resources, the use of energy during production and transport, by-product emissions either as solids, gases or liquids, and the longevity of any product in both its useful and waste states. These are the issues we need to consider when choosing and evaluating items for our homes.

The realization that nearly every object used in making and furnishing our homes has an impact on the environment makes the need for ecologically sound choices all too clear. There are essentially two positive approaches we can adopt in order to make safe, healthy homes and protect the planet. We can take inspiration from traditional techniques of building that have proved safe for centuries and existed before the industrial revolution. And we can seek out the growing number of exciting new products that are starting to be developed by a new, twenty-first century industrial revolution. These 'clean' processes imitate nature's closed-loop cycles to avoid resource depletion, pollution and waste. Such methods make cleaner, safer artefacts that are the way to healthier homes – and a healthier planet.

TRADITIONAL AND MODERN

This old ladderback chair (above) is made of simple local materials and displays all the characteristics of traditional benign design. The bent plywood chair with chromed steel legs (left) is attractive, but it has many of the poor environmental credentials typical of first industrial age, non-sustainable production.

FALLING WATER

In his building 'Falling Water' (previous pages), architect Frank Lloyd Wright used natural materials to create a home that is in harmony with its surroundings.

ENERGY AND POLLUTION

OUR LIFESTYLES TODAY RELY ON CHEAP ENERGY that comes from easily tapped fossil fuels. We use products derived from oil not only for light, warmth and power, but also to power the vehicles that move us around and for the production of the things we use. If measured in real terms, however, this energy costs the earth very dear. Burning fossil fuel depletes the earth's natural resources and causes toxic emissions to the atmosphere and the pollution of land and water. It also distorts the earth's naturally balanced climate patterns by damaging forests and oceans. Furthermore, cheap energy facilitates cheap production, and thus high levels of consumption. The consequences of this are further expenditure of natural resources, the generation of more polluting emissions and the creation of ever greater volumes of waste. As well as decorating safely, it is essential to decorate with less.

The earth's stock of mineral resources is finite. Oil, gas and coal have taken many millions of years to form. Exact estimates vary, but at current rates it is likely that the world's oil will last only to about the year 2050, natural gas until 2030, and coal until 2200. While there may be hidden reserves, extracting these more remote stocks becomes self defeating because the more inaccessible they are, the greater the energy needed to extract them. It would be unrealistic to maintain that none of the world's resources should be used at all, but those that are must come from properly managed sources. And more of the energy we use should derive from the earth's natural, renewable and clean sources – the sun, wind and oceans.

PETROCHEMICAL PRODUCTS

A by-product of the growth in energy consumption has been the burgeoning petrochemical industry, which now produces some 95 per cent of all the chemicals in use today. These contain petrochemical derivatives, many of which are dangerous to our health. Many petrochemical-based products, of which plastics are the most commonly used examples, are harmful, even though they may appear safe. Petrochemical molecules (carbon) combine easily with many other chemicals – very often chlorine which is extremely dangerous – to produce a vast range of new substances. These produce many toxic emissions and useless, polluting wastes. When disposed of, these wastes emit further atmospheric, liquid and solid pollutants.

AIR POLLUTION

Atmospheric pollution causes extensive environmental degradation. By far the most damaging chemical emissions are carbon monoxide, carbon dioxide, sulphuric acid and nitrous oxide, which, together with chlorine, contribute to the destruction of atmospheric ozone as well as disturbing the world's self-regulating climate systems. In nature, these substances exist in small, finely balanced quantities in the earth's ecological system – a balance that is disturbed by the huge quantities produced by industry and households. About 26 per cent of greenhouse gases are created by households.

Carbon dioxide is increasing in the atmosphere. The build-up acts like a huge blanket over the earth, trapping its heat and thereby causing global warming and affecting weather patterns. Every one of us contributes to this – Londoners, for example, each generate about ten tonnes of carbon dioxide a year.

Carbon monoxide is emitted by the incomplete combustion of fossil fuels for home heating and lighting, as well as manufacturing and transport. It is colourless and odourless but deadly because it inhibits the healthy functioning of human and animal organs and blood cells. It can be a killer when inhaled in confined spaces. It is estimated that the average human adds three tonnes of carbon monoxide a year to the atmosphere by means of the energy consumed by transport, heating and lighting.

A NATURAL LANDSCAPE
Air, light, soil, water and plant growth are all part of nature's self-regulating, cyclical system, which is threatened by human impact on the earth.

Sulphur dioxide is given off during many industrial processes and becomes sulphuric acid when in contact with atmospheric moisture. Like nitrous oxide, it produces acid rain, damaging soil, waterways, lakes and forests as well as creating photochemical fogs. Studies have found increases in childhood cancer and cardiac failure in areas of high sulphur oxide pollution.

Nitrous oxide reacts with the volatile organic compounds (VOCs) present in many decorating products, to generate ozone which is dangerous at low levels and cause a range of irritations. At upper atmospheric levels, where the ozone naturally remains largely constant, the ozone layer protects all life from the sun's harmful radiation. But when volatile organic compounds (chemicals such as methyl chloroform, marbon tetrachloride, halons and methyl bromides) react with sunlight, they produce chlorine, which destroys the ozone layer much more rapidly than the earth naturally generates it. Provided that international agreements to reduce ozone-destroying emissions are adhered to, this destruction might be repaired within about 50 years.

WATER POLLUTION

Waterways are polluted by toxic emissions from many processes, including the washing and cooling of mechanical

equipment, the washing of fabrics and paper during production, and pesticide run-off from sheep and cotton. The fast-growing microchip industry, in particular, discharges huge quantities of water polluted with toxins. Water is also polluted by chemicals leaching from waste in landfill sites.

SOLID WASTE AND LAND POLLUTION

Solid waste is no less a concern. In the USA, it is said that every kilogram of produce delivered to consumers results in 28 kilograms of waste material – much of it containing dangerous chemicals. Worldwide, the ratio averages at one unit of product to eight units of waste. Only a small proportion of the by-products of manufacturing processes can be absorbed by the earth's natural biodegrading systems. The rest must be stored away in landfill sites, where it pollutes the underlying ground and water and generates polluting gas as it decomposes. If incinerated rather than dumped, waste emits yet more dangerous chemicals, such as dioxins, into the atmosphere, which can damage health. For example, mothers living near waste

incinerators have been shown to have a higher than normal level of contaminants in their breast milk.

DOMESTIC POLLUTION

What we do in our homes makes a significant contribution to the ill health of the planet. There are three main types of action we can take to reduce this impact. First, we can choose – and thus encourage manufacturers to make – products and materials that do not cause environmental damage. Second, we can modify our patterns of consumption so that we encourage less production, use fewer resources and so reduce the amount of waste. Homes can be as – or even more – comfortable and attractive while consuming and containing less. The global environment will improve if everyone follows the '3R' rules – Reduce, Repair, Recycle. Third, we can take measures to reduce the amount of energy consumed by our homes.

The UK Building Research Establishment has shown that of the chemicals commonly used in building materials, 41 cause climate change, 18 cause ozone depletion, 85 create photochemical ozone, 7 create acid rain, 120 cause toxic emissions to air and 53 to water. The effects of these chemicals are not confined to global pollution: they also adversely affect the quality of the air inside our homes, and thus our health.

SAFE DESIGN

Built with materials taken from its woodland setting, this room (top) displays many features of safe design. The stove also uses local, renewable wood as a fuel.

DESIGNING WITH LESS

This minimalist bathroom (above) is a perfect example of how designing with less can create a powerful, positive look.

Reduce, Reuse, Recycle

HOME AND HEALTH

This home was constructed according to ecologically sound principles. It is safe both for the environment and its occupants.

THE LINKS BETWEEN FURNISHING and decorating materials to the quality of our indoor environments are no less strong than their links to the global environment. In the industrialized world, we spend as much as 90 per cent of our time indoors, so the importance of healthy indoor air cannot be overestimated. Yet the quality of indoor air can be ten times worse than that of external air – even in urban areas. We therefore need to minimize indoor air pollution and ensure that our homes have plenty of fresh air and natural light.

The Environmental Protection Agency (EPA) in the United States considers poor indoor air quality one of the greatest single factors contributing to ill health, but this fact has scarcely been acknowledged, until recently. Studies of indoor environments suggest that many modern materials and chemicals contribute to a growing catalogue of illnesses. It is also estimated that the many potentially harmful chemicals in our homes can be up to 1,600 times more potent when combined with others.

Apart from a small range of bad odours, there are few indicators of poor indoor air quality. But just because we don't smell them does not mean that pollutants are not present. Just as foods contain an increasing number of tasteless but harmful additives, modern materials, too, are made up of a complex mixtures of chemical ingredients. Our homes are filled with potential dangers from a wide range of unsuspected sources. These include:

▶ Carpets glued with solvents, treated with fungicides and containing residual pesticides
▶ Fabrics treated with chlorine, benzine and formaldehyde
▶ Plywoods and other common particle boards that contain formaldehyde, urea and other dangerous glues
▶ Paints and stains that contain fungicides, volatile organic compounds (VOCs) and other chemicals
▶ Vinyl flooring, foam furniture and plastics that contain VOCs such as bromines and chlorine
▶ Cleaning materials, cosmetics and garden pesticides

EXTRA SPACE

A conservatory acts as an additional room, draught lobby and solar heat collector.

NATURAL PAINT

Walls and ceilings near windows are painted in light tones using organic, vegetable-based paints.

EFFICIENT HEATING

Radiator positioned in the middle of the living space for more efficient heat distribution.

SAFE UNITS

Kitchen units are made of plywood with a granite worktop instead of the usual laminates and particle boards.

RECYCLED MATERIALS

Floor made of reclaimed oak boards. Structural columns are debarked, but untreated tree trunks.

Yet humans have inhabited homes for centuries without such problems. This may be because traditional homes were usually made with materials taken from the immediate surroundings – chemical-free timbers, fabrics coloured with natural plant dyes, wood finishes containing beeswax, floors from local stone. But new materials have radically altered our home environment and our bodies are ill equipped to cope with the impact of the chemicals they contain, many of which, as we have seen, give off pollutants.

Fortunately, most people have immune systems that are strong enough cope with toxic stress, but the longer we are exposed to this onslaught, or the less sound our immune system, the greater the likelihood of ill health. The alarming growth of many illnesses would seem to bear out this theory: asthma, allergenic reactions, respiratory ailments and diseases, and cancers were not present in such numbers in previous generations.

INDOOR AIR QUALITY

Two factors have coincided to create the dangerous indoor air quality common today. The first is the development of new materials used in the construction of homes since the end of World War II. Cheap, quickly built mass housing exploited the new, often lightweight materials and processes offered by the developing petrochemical industry. Many of these materials release chemicals into the air – a process called offgassing.

The second factor was the determination, since the 1970s, to conserve energy. This had two consequences. First, energy consumption was reduced by increasing insulation in buildings, using mainly petrochemical products such as foamed polymeric insulation materials. This was coupled with a drive to seal houses tightly and prevent the loss of all the warm air that we heat with such high energy costs. Fireplaces and all the draughty nooks and

A HEALTHY HOME
This modern home (far left) has plenty of light without excessive glazing, windows on either side of the space for cross ventilation, a timber floor that is easy to keep clean, and indoor plants to help regulate indoor air quality

OUTDOOR LIVING SPACE
Natural, safe building materials are used in this semi-outdoor living space (left). With fresh air and light as well as sufficient cover and shade, it provides an ideal link between interior and outdoor environments.

crannies were blocked up, eliminating ventilation. This sealed in not only human-generated germs, toxins and moisture but also the vast number of chemicals that are vaporized and offgassed into the home's now unchanging air. Indoor air, stagnant for longer periods than outdoor air, spiralled down in quality. So-called advanced building technology has created home environments with previously unknown dangers. It has taken some twenty or more years for these problems to be fully appreciated.

CAUSES OF POOR INDOOR AIR QUALITY

Poor indoor air has four main causes: offgassing of chemicals from materials, particulates, combustion gases, and electro-magnetic radiation. The presence of these in the air can trigger a variety of physiological reactions such as eye, nose and throat irritations, fatigue, headaches, respiratory disorders and allergenic reactions. For a list of the more common chemicals used in paints and adhesives and some of their suspected health effects, see p.180.

▶ Offgassing (or outgassing) from materials is the slow release into the atmosphere – similar to evaporation – of chemicals that vaporize either from the material itself, or from chemical residues used in manufacturing processes. The chemicals may be naturally unstable or may be released through aging or by the effect of light, moisture or abrasion. Chemicals commonly emitted into the atmosphere in this way include the dangerous group known as volatile organic compounds (VOCs) and many other petrochemical derivatives, such as benzine, naptha, formaldehyde, organochlorines, phenols and the organophosphates contained in PVCs. Toxic metals such as lead, mercury, cadmium and zinc also offgas, and they can cause particularly severe contamination if they come into contact with water or other particulates. Materials commonly used in the home that usually contain these chemicals are plywoods, particleboards, insulation, carpets, vinyl flooring adhesives, paints and fabrics.

▶ Particulate and biological contaminants are important contributors to poor indoor air. The air in all homes contains airborne particles that are so fine they are invisible; the more common of these are general household dust, animal fibres, microorganisms, pollens and mould spores as well as smoke and asbestos. Moulds in particular can be poisonous. Particles can trigger a range of reactions, including eczema and hay fever, and the restriction of breathing passages that causes asthma and respiratory problems. The World Health Organization (WHO) maintains that the threshold below which particulates are safe is so low as to be barely measurable. A WHO survey suggests that 6 per cent of all deaths in Europe are the result of lung problems caused by particles.

▶ Combustion gases can be emitted by old, faulty or badly maintained appliances. These may burn their fuels only partially and so emit gaseous residues such as nitrogen dioxide, carbon monoxide and sulphur dioxide, into the air. Carbon monoxide in the home can kill and leads to a large number of symptoms often assumed to be those of influenza. Current research has shown that carbon mon-oxide can impair cognitive functions, and has also revealed links with lung disease. Appliances should be tested to make sure that they are burning properly.

▶ Electromagnetic fields are perhaps the most contentious of domestic hazards. Electricity and electrical installations surround us in increasing density, and there is growing concern that these fields upset many of the body's finely balanced natural electrochemical functions. There are two kinds of radiation: low-frequency electrical fields emitted from electric cables and equipment, and the magnetic fields emitted from all appliances and equipment – these are considered the most dangerous (see pp.102–5). So extensive is the growing evidence against them that the Swedish and Russian governments have begun to legislate in order to protect people from potential dangers.

Despite all these problems, there are ways of making homes that are healthy to live in and do as little damage as possible to the environment. The following lists the main strategies, all of which are explained later in this book.

▶ Minimize energy consumption in your home to reduce consumption of fossil fuels.

▶ Decorate in a style that uses fewer rather than more things and purchase these locally.

▶ Choose benign materials, old or new, that do not damage the environment: the less processing a material has undergone, the safer it is likely to be.

▶ Select materials that do not offgas and damage indoor air quality.

▶ Ensure that all boilers, cookers and fires are properly serviced and maintained.

▶ Ventilate interiors to ensure constant fresh air, using a range of non-mechanical techniques.

▶ Make your home as light and as noise-free as possible.

▶ Use plants to counteract indoor pollution.

A SIMPLE INTERIOR

In this home made of local, renewable and biodegradable materials, rich textures combine with deliberately sparse furnishings to create a calm, attractive space (left).

OLD AND NEW

Traditional and modern elements sit comfortably together in this living room (below). Stone floors create a visual link to the outside and store solar heat. Natural, unplastered walls set off the bold timber structure and the delicacy of some of the furniture.

TRADITIONAL DESIGN

PRE-INDUSTRIAL MATERIALS AND DESIGNS are generally more environmentally sound than materials developed by modern industrial processes. Now, at the beginning of the twenty-first century, we are realizing that lessons can be learned from the design principles of earlier, pre-industrial cultures. Much of the attraction, as well as the benign environmental consequences, of vernacular, or ordinary domestic, design comes from its simplicity. Traditional cultures husbanded resources by using the simplest materials and forms – a philosophy expressed by the modern slogans 'form follows function' and 'less is more'. Design does not need to be complex to be beautiful.

VERNACULAR STYLES
Vernacular approaches to homemaking have unwittingly embodied principles that are essentially kind to the environment and these are still valid today: materials were obtained locally and used with care; they were natural, renewable and safe when discarded. Basic but effective methods were used to heat and ventilate interiors. While in modern homes this is done using energy-greedy equipment, vernacular builders exploit the qualities of local materials for their climate-modifying benefits. In desert areas, for example, thick walls made of local mud keep interior temperatures cool by absorbing the sun's heat, while in the cool nights the warm walls radiate some of the heat absorbed during the day into the house. In northern forested countries, roofs of solid logs are covered with grass and act as efficient insulators, while in the forested tropics, open timber-frame construction lets cooling breezes into homes.

Traditional materials that have stood the test of time still satisfy us with their unsophisticated beauty. Simple, unadorned interiors are so much more than an assembly of fashionable shapes and colours. The lasting qualities of natural materials, such as stone flags, terracotta tiles and wooden walls, come partly from their connection with the local landscape and local skills, as well as the meanings and messages they carry about the continuing traditions of homemaking.

By contrast, many of today's homes lack this sense of coherence and belonging to their surroundings. Instead, they are a product of a 'pick and mix' approach to design, made possible by widely available materials that are

ROUGH-HEWN STONE
Natural materials left unadorned link a home to its natural context.

BAMBOO
Safe and renewable, bamboo is a distinctive material.

TIMBER
Wood is strong, safe, renewable and a good insulator.

BRICK AND FLINT
Brick and flint are characteristic building materials in eastern England.

PART OF THE LANDSCAPE

These Norwegian homes derive their beauty from environmentally sound building principles and the use of local materials. Log walls and earth-covered roofs provide excellent insulation and create dwellings that are part of the landscape. Likewise, the interior of the Frank Lloyd Wright house 'Falling Water' (below) shows the bold use of local materials that tie the building to its surroundings.

VERSATILE CORK

Cork, shown before processing, is a versatile, renewable material, used for floor and wall coverings (below).

PART OF THE ENVIRONMENT

This glazed-in dining area with a floor made of local wood blends well with its surroundings (right).

transported from all over the world. The mass production and standardization of new homes leaves little room for regional variation – for those enjoyable differences between one house and another. This eclectic post-modern approach may be fashionable at the moment, but the almost universal admiration for traditional styles suggests that most of us have a need for the kind of permanence and connection to local context enjoyed by our ancestors. The use of traditional techniques and materials is one way of regaining this joy.

Clearly, the idea of using only local materials cannot be sustained in today's global economy, but the concept of 'appropriate' materials is still valid. For example, in areas where wood is a common construction material, wooden flooring will strike a happier note than materials from elsewhere – marble or mosaic, however beautiful, may seem out of place. Appropriateness to context remains a guiding principle for selection of materials, but we need to add to this the principle of minimum environmental impact. However appropriate the material, we must

ensure that other aspects, such as its production and transport, are environmentally benign. While these ideas further narrow the range of choice, they suggest an expansion of traditional principles to fit today's global world.

One of the most difficult of such issues is that of employment conditions. If we apply the same criteria that we value in our society to production conditions in less developed countries, we expand the old concept of constructive local employment into today's global context. An example might be a retailer of home furnishing in the developed world who insists that his third-world suppliers reduce child working hours and provide some schooling and health care, which he, the retailer, subsidizes. If buying power in the developed world increases the trade of such manufacturers, then others will be obliged to follow, creating a benign circle.

ORIGINAL ARTS AND CRAFTS
This classic Lutyens Arts and Crafts interior shows a sophisticated interpretation of English vernacular building, using local raw brick and solid oak for the structure, finishes and furniture (above left).

A NEW APPROACH

However much we might wish to return to vernacular designs, simply deploying modern materials to emulate their performance is not enough. Traditional design must be augmented to include new materials and technologies whose benefits cannot be ignored. Aspects of production that were viable in the pre-industrial age must now be updated for the twenty-first century.

MODERN ARTS AND CRAFTS
A modern version of the Arts and Crafts style still incorporates solid and durable materials and avoids superfluous decoration (above).

NEW TECHNOLOGY

IMAGINATIVE SCIENTISTS AND MANUFACTURERS NOW REALIZE that the destructive patterns of most nineteenth- and twentieth-century industries are unsustainable. These first industrial revolution processes are linear and dirty: they take the earth's natural resources and use large amounts of energy to make a product, producing waste that can be so dangerous as to render unusable other parts of nature's potential resources. But we are at the dawn of a second industrial revolution, in which new, clean production methods that copy the earth's organic processes are employed. These are cyclical, using safe, renewable resources that are organically generated. Most waste goes toward regeneration of new products – just like waste food becomes compost for growing more plants. The environmental aspects of these new processes include:

▶ The replacement of petrochemical products with naturally occurring ones that are non-hazardous, unprocessed and preferably renewable, such as natural paints and lime plasters, and linoleum and cork floors.

▶ The use of raw materials from the maximum number of species of plant or types of resource in order to spread the impact and allow regeneration.

▶ The use of raw materials located close to production.

▶ The use of renewable energy, such as solar and wind power, and of heat recovery techniques in processing equipment, to allow the recycling of energy.

▶ The extension of product life by the disassembly and reuse of components, and recycling.

▶ The recycling of waste to provide the ingredients of secondary and even tertiary products

This new 'benign' approach to manufacturing processes is sometimes referred to as 'biomimicry' and it has great potential for a safer future. Some of the environmentally benign materials now being made in this way include

DIRTY INDUSTRY/LINEAR MANUFACTURING

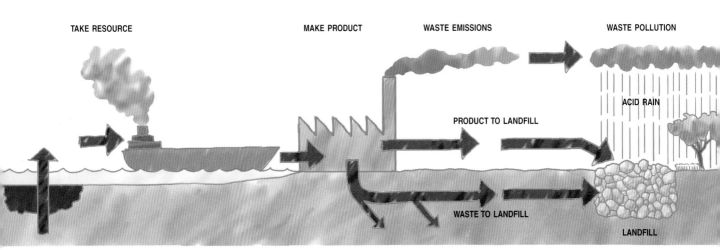

TAKE RESOURCE   MAKE PRODUCT   WASTE EMISSIONS   WASTE POLLUTION

ACID RAIN

PRODUCT TO LANDFILL

WASTE TO LANDFILL

LANDFILL

OIL RESOURCE

This illustrates the linear, non-sustainable processes bequeathed by the Industrial Revolution.

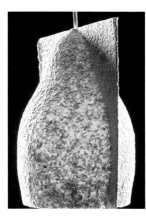

RECYCLED SHADE

This lamp shade (left) has been made from paper pulp produced from recycled paper.

'CLEAN' TEXTILES

These fabrics have been made with closed-loop processes that avoid polluting emissions and chemical residues.

carpets from recycled plastic bottles, paints made from vegetable extracts, tiles from crushed ceramic waste, rubber flooring from recycled tyres, plastic from plant-based cellulose, and self-coloured cottons that need no additional dyes.

Typical of these new, clean products are Climatex Lifecycle™ fabrics, which have set new, high standards of environmental safety. Produced by the pioneering company DesignTex, the fabrics are made from worsted wool and ramie – both biodegradable yarns. DesignTex surveyed

8,000 potential chemicals for use and found only 38 that were considered sufficiently free from known or suspected toxic or otherwise dangerous effects. The fabric gradually decays and provides organic nutrients in the same way as any biodegradable waste – the trimmings are used by farmers instead of plastic for weed-suppressing cover. The DesignTex factory in Switzerland also claims that all water used in its processes is cleaned to drinking quality before being returned to rivers. The company has become a model for manufacturers worldwide.

SUSTAINABLE INDUSTRY/CLOSED-LOOP CYCLE

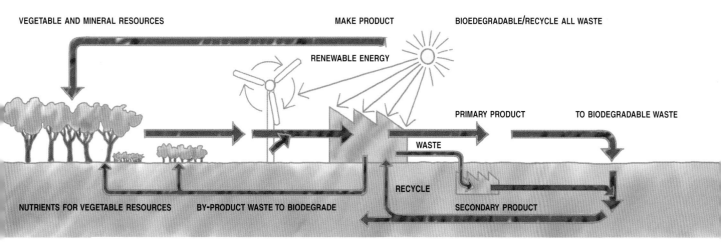

This illustrates the principles of 'clean' sustainable processes that emulate nature's closed-loop cycles.

While the range of such products is small at present, it is growing as manufacturers begin to realize that, in the long-term, clean processing will prove more, rather than less, profitable. Together with the general acceptance of the still untapped potential of renewable energy, this is an enormously positive sign for the future.

Creative re-evaluation of modern production is also leading to a new look at patterns of trade. Some companies are beginning to think in wider environmental terms — one plants trees to absorb the same amount of carbon dioxide as it pumps into the air through transport of its goods. An international carpet company now leases instead of sells its product to the customer. Credit is given for the worn carpet, which is taken away and recycled to make a lower-grade product to be sold to another customer, and so on. There is a shift towards the idea of providing services rather than products, creating the attitude — 'don't own it, use it'

SOURCING ETHICAL PRODUCERS

Twenty-first-century technology makes clean production possible. It also makes it easier for us to find out about the products we use. The Internet now gives everyone access to information, making it possible to check the chemical ingredients of a product or the environmental credentials of almost any company. Details of the methods used by a Californian furniture workshop or a Swiss textile mill, for example, will never make the shelves of your local library, but this kind of information is increasingly available at the click of a mouse. As more and more businesses post details of their products on the Internet, finding the nearest, safest or least polluting source of an item becomes ever easier.

Exposing the polluting practices of manufacturers is another important element of this growing source of environmental information. Many government agencies — both central and local — keep track of the activities of companies and publicize any breaches of environmental controls. This has two effects: first, it becomes harder for companies to hide poor environmental policies; second, the process of naming and shaming may force companies to clean up their environmental performance. They may do so for economic reasons, but what counts in the end is that they damage the environment less.

The Internet also makes scrutiny of ethical performance possible. In the new global supermarket, the buying power of each and every individual is one of the few significant

SUSTAINABLE FOREST
Bamboo is a durable, sustainable material that grows six times faster than most hardwoods (far left).

CALIFORNIAN WINDFARM
Generating electricity from renewable resources avoids the depletion of fossil fuels (left).

ETHICAL CONSIDERATIONS
Importers of goods from developing countries need to look closely at working practices in order to ensure ethical labour conditions during production (below).

constraints on unscrupulous corporations: if no one buys tropical hardwoods, the rainforest will survive; if no one uses PVC products or paints that are high in VOCs, significant toxic emissions will be reduced. This has been demonstrated by a campaign mounted by student organizations, labour unions and other concerned groups in the USA to improve the extremely poor working conditions in the international garment industry. They formed the Fair Labour Association, which insists on certain employment standards in factories around the world. If manufacturers do not treat their employees fairly, their survival is threatened through negative publicity on the Internet. Garments made by factories that comply with the regulations now carry the Fair Labour Association's label.

Today we can combine the timeless functionalism of traditional design and techniques with the products of new, clean technology and develop a safe ecological style. Instead of selecting materials that simply reflect current fashions, selection can be based on the realities behind every material or product – from its source through its whole lifecycle. This benign design approach will create individual homes in tune with their context, which will keep you safe and not degrade the planet.

EVALUATING MATERIALS

OW CAN WE SELECT MATERIALS THAT ARE SAFE both for personal and environmental health? The issues touched on so far demonstrate that every material or product needs to satisfy criteria about its source, manufacture, health consequences and behaviour as waste. Because few decorating materials carry eco-labels, we need a set of questions to ask suppliers and manufacturers about their products.

Environmental issues are so multifaceted that despite the considerable research taking place, no absolute safety standard has been established. The organizations that have developed eco-labelling systems (see pp.194–5) all apply different criteria. But while experts argue about differences of detail, all agree on the main issues. These form the basis of the charts detailing the environmental credentials of some of the materials discussed in chapter three:

► The depletion of natural resources caused by the making of a product
► The amount of energy consumed in the production or processing of a product – called its embodied energy
► The amount of pollutants emitted during manufacture
► A product's impact on indoor air quality and health
► A product's ability to biodegrade harmlessly, or its potential for recycling
► Ethical issues affecting the community that makes a product

DEPLETION OF NATURAL RESOURCES

The issue here is the extent to which the extraction of a material exhausts the supply of that material for future generations. The stock of natural resources, other than those regenerated through vegetable growth, is finite and strategies are needed to reorientate production to make use of renewable resources – many of which are fuelled by the sun's energy. But the extraction of even some of these resources may have damaging environmental consequences that warrant protection of the resource. For example, hardwoods from tropical rainforests can be regrown –

CORK HARVEST

In some areas of the Mediterranean, cork harvesting is a staple industry. Buying habits in the rest of the world can affect the stability of these local communities.

albeit slowly. But their loss deprives unique flora and fauna of their habitats, as well as possibly causing earth erosion. The forests in which these trees grow also provide the earth's greatest 'sponge' for absorbing greenhouse gases.

EMBODIED ENERGY

This is the amount of energy consumed by extracting the raw materials for a product, including all aspects of its processing, manufacture and transport. Transport from point of sale to point of use must also be considered.

POLLUTING EMISSIONS

The amount of polluting waste that is emitted into the atmosphere, land or water during the manufacture of a product. This includes pollution from burning fossil fuels. It is important to note the simple rule that the closer a material remains to its natural state, the less processing will be involved, hence the smaller the burden on the environment.

INDOOR AIR QUALITY

This evaluates the impact that materials have on indoor air and therefore our health. While there are many different ways in which materials can affect indoor air quality, for practical purposes these are grouped together. Even if a material has little impact from many environmental aspects, one potentially harmful effect makes it unsatisfactory.

RECYCLING POTENTIAL AND WASTE GENERATION

These issues relate to the ability of a material or product to biodegrade safely or be recycled when it has completed its useful life. Recycling can take three forms: first, an item, such as a door or window, can be reused in its original state; second, it may be reprocessed to form new materials (for example, plastic bottles can be reprocessed to become the fibres for carpets); third, the item may be disassembled and its components reused.

ETHICAL ISSUES

The demand for cheap goods in the developed world has huge social consequences and can lead to hopelessly inadequate working conditions – even slavery – in developing areas. It is vital to evaluate manufacturers' attention to

SLATE QUARRYING
Slate is a safe material that can be used time and time again (above)

CLAY TILES
These roof tiles are made from local clay dug from the ground (right).

matters such as child labour, fair wages, health and safety issues and education. Ask questions and look for labels that certify acceptable standards (see pp. 194–5).

OTHER FACTORS

Each material and every instance in which it is used will raise particular issues that cannot be generalized. If any assessment of environmental and health issues is to be meaningful in your own circumstances, there will be additional, specific questions to ask. Most common are: the methods and materials used for packing; the dangers posed by work on the material outside factory conditions; onerous cleaning requirements; the impact on individuals with particular health sensitivities.

Everyone is likely to place weight on different criteria, and developing a set of individual priorities will lead to very personal selections. In so doing, you will create a home that is not only safer for the environment and your health, but also expresses your own personality and values.

RECYCLED PLASTICS

This practical table top (below) is
made from recycled plastic bottles.

Chapter Two

LIGHT, HEAT AND AIR

LIGHT

THE PLAY OF LIGHT ON SURFACES, SHAPES AND TEXTURES creates the beauty of space. Light casts shadows, gives definition to form and creates mood and atmosphere in a room. The manipulation of light is one of the most powerful tools in making successful interiors.

Without light, life would not exist. Like plants, humans depend on light as a source of energy – both directly and indirectly, all living things are driven by light from the sun. For humans, this dependence is not only physiological but also emotional – sunlight cheers, greyness depresses. For a home to be healthy and feel happy and comfortable, it needs as much natural light as possible.

The importance of natural light tends to be forgotten today, when electricity allows us to work 24 hours a day, even at times when our biological clocks are urging us to sleep. As a species, humans evolved to function according to the rhythms of outdoor light, yet many of us now spend as much as 90 per cent of our time indoors, effectively in permanent gloom. Light is measured in units called lux. One lux is the equivalent of the light of one candle. A bright, sunny day measures up to 80,000 lux and even an overcast grey sky is up to about 10,000 lux. In contrast, the recommended level of light for working indoors is between 300 and 500 lux, and general light levels in our homes are usually about 250 lux.

Our need for natural light is illustrated by accumulating evidence of the effects of low levels of light on health. One example is the condition known as SAD – Seasonal Affective Disorder – which affects people living in northern latitudes, where winter days are short and light levels are low for months at a time. SAD causes severe depression and lethargy in sufferers, but can be relieved by regular doses of bright light from a specially designed light box. These boxes contain full spectrum lights – lights that are as close as possible to natural daylight.

The message for the homemaker is simple: your home, both literally and metaphorically, should be as light and sunny as possible. Unless there are pressing problems such as damp, my priority is always to increase the amount of light in a home and to use decorative effects to enhance apparent brightness. In many homes, great improvements in light levels can be made with small amounts of self-contained building work that need cause little disruption.

BRING LIGHT INTO YOUR HOME

There is a distinction between sunlight and daylight. Sunlight is direct sun, while daylight is cast by the sky – and is received either directly or indirectly. Each has its own colour qualities and intensity.

Sky brightness and sunlight angles vary according to location. The higher the sun in the sky, the brighter and hotter are its rays. In northern European countries, sunlight angles are much lower than those in southern Europe and most of North America. Although weaker and less hot, low-angled sunlight penetrates deeper into a room – a benefit in northern latitudes. In areas with higher sun angles and strong heat, screening and filtering light becomes more important to protect the home from too much brightness at midday and in high summer.

Traditional buildings all over the world have an array of devices for controlling the amount of light entering a building. Regardless of the numerous variations in design, however, there are four main ways of making the best use of light:

▶ Allocate rooms to maximize natural light at different times of day.
▶ Add transparency – create views from one room to another.
▶ Increase the amount of light coming into the dwelling.
▶ Use reflected light.
▶ Add screens of various kinds to modify or filter light coming into rooms.

The role of glass is fundamental in creating light in the home and for controlling heat loss and gain. It also offers a wealth of decorative opportunities. For more details on the practical aspects of using glass, see pp.140–143.

POSITIONING ROOMS

▶ Look at how the sun travels around your home and, if possible, match the use of rooms to the sun's path. For example, bedrooms should face east to catch the morning sun, and living rooms south or west to receive afternoon and early morning sun. Use darker rooms least frequently or possibly only at night.

▶ Don't assume that a room previously designated a living- or bedroom must always be used as such. You will get great pleasure every day waking up in a sun-filled east-facing room, even if it is smaller than a north-facing room that your predecessors made their master bedroom.

ADDING TRANSPARENCY

▶ Windows in internal walls or glazed screens between areas can illuminate one space by 'borrowing' light from another. If privacy is needed, use screens of opaque glass, which cast a diffuse light, or hang blinds to cover clear glass. Japanese designers have mastered the art of creating soft, diffused light by using rice paper *shoji* screens, which have a calming, peaceful effect.

▶ Extra areas of transparency within a dwelling bring a feeling of light and space. Solid walls can stop short of meeting at corners and the gap can be filled by a strip of glass. This will allow light from one room into another

SCREENED LIGHT

Translucent screens allow a soft, gentle light to permeate from the room beyond. Although separate, the spaces are visually connected by the light.

and create the sculptural impression of walls floating in space. Maximum effect is gained by setting the glass into the wall surface without any frame, and treating different wall planes with different colours or textures. Art Nouveau interiors are particularly rich in transparency, using internal screens and coloured glass to give spaces a warm, glowing richness.

▶ Glimpses of sunlight on walls or floors seen from north-facing rooms will significantly improve the sense of brightness. Do this simply by changing a solid door into one with glazing, and use blinds or opaque, sand-blasted or acid-etched glass for privacy.

INCREASING LIGHT

▶ With relatively minor building works, windows can be altered, bringing radical improvements to a home. For example, it is reasonably easy to lower a windowsill and create a full-length window that allows light to flood the floor and reflect up into the room.

▶ The higher a window, the more light it will throw into the room. Increase the height of existing windows or, in a high-ceilinged room, add small, high windows as separate clerestories. These do not need to be opened, so they can be made simply of glass set in frames. They can be left unobstructed, even when lower windows are curtained.

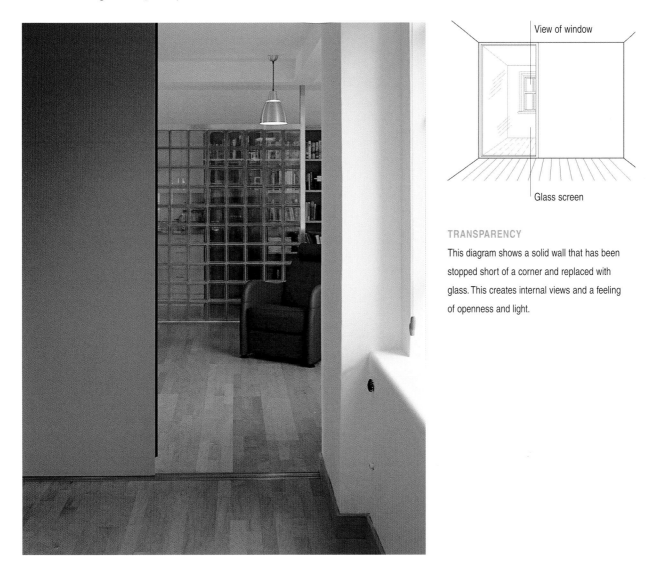

View of window

Glass screen

TRANSPARENCY

This diagram shows a solid wall that has been stopped short of a corner and replaced with glass. This creates internal views and a feeling of openness and light.

Black-painted window frames act like picture frames to draw the eye into the garden (left). The connection between inside and out is further emphasized by the continuous, light-reflecting flooring.

ROOFLIGHT

A mirrored wall next to the skylight maximizes the light in this cosy attic room and makes the space seem double the size (above). The timber surround reflects a warm, soft light,

Oriole

Square bay

Existing opening

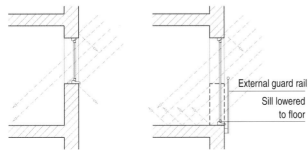

External guard rail

Sill lowered to floor

Without altering the structure of a window opening, it is possible to add an oriole window or a square bay projecting out from the wall to create a light-filled extension to the room (left). An attractive seat can be added in a bay window.

▶ The shape of a window can be changed without altering the structural opening in the wall. Replace a flat window with either a square projecting bay or an oriole (see above). This can make a light-filled area and, if the sill is low enough, a window seat.

▶ Use skylights to brighten dark areas at the top of a house. Because the light from the sky directly overhead is so much brighter than the light from the horizon, even a small skylight is highly effective. Anyone with the good fortune to be on the top floor of an apartment building should try to obtain permission to install skylights. Make sure that these are double or triple glazed to prevent condensation from rising warm air.

▶ On upper floors or in flats – if permission can be obtained – an excellent way to create a feeling of airiness is to make inward-opening French windows down to the floor and protect the opening with a set of railings for safety. These 'Romeo and Juliet' balconies are common in many traditional European buildings and transform even the dullest room into one that is filled with light.

▶ Simple to install are 'light tubes' – these are small tubular skylights, some only 300 mm in diameter, which work on the same principle as a periscope. They can bend to funnel bright daylight from the opening at roof level

ROMEO AND JULIET BALCONY

The easiest part of a window to alter is the wall beneath the sill. Removing the sill beneath a window and installing French doors will make the whole room feel like a balcony and allow light to enter the room and bounce off the floor. A protective railing is placed outside the wall line for safety. These structures are sometimes called Romeo and Juliet balconies (left).

down into a space. Light tubes can be taken through two floors – although finding a route is not always easy.

▶ Tiny glass inserts no larger than one or two bricks set in outside walls bring in shafts of light and can greatly enliven a gloomy interior. Sixteenth-century Turkish bathhouses had roofs inset with glass lenses, creating wonderful diffused light. A master of the art of bringing daylight to interiors was the English architect John

Soane. He used hidden skylights to throw light onto richly coloured wall surfaces, often reflecting it in mirrors to create spaces of infinite luminosity, even in the darkest interiors.

▶ One of the best ways to create a light-filled room is to add a conservatory. Conservatories can be truly sunny semi-outdoor spaces and can also function as a valuable source of heat from solar gain (see pp.66–8).

A CALMING LIGHT

This large space is suffused with an even light that is characteristic of north-facing rooflights (left). Light enters from two opposite sides of the room, creating an atmosphere of balanced calm.

A VARIETY OF EFFECTS

Different sizes and styles of window give very different light effects in this room (right). A large opening on the left gives general illumination while a small glass inset in the wall provides a sharp focus of light. A delicate sparkle of points of light comes from the pierced screen on the far wall.

REFLECTED LIGHT

▶ Maximize the effect of whatever natural light does enter your room by keeping floor surfaces near the window light in colour so that they bounce daylight deep into the room. However, if you have a solid floor you may want to use dark colours on surfaces near windows so that the floor absorbs heat (see p.66).

▶ Light furnishings and other flat surfaces such as table tops near the window, give a greater impression of light than darker colours.

▶ Glazing bars, which divide a window into smaller panes, can add to the luminescence in a space. Light bounces off them and so increases the apparent brightness. Traditional white painted glazing bars and Venetian blinds create this feeling of lightness – provided they are slender enough. Many modern windows lose this quality because the glazing bars are too thick.

▶ The window surround (or cheeks) is important for reflecting light into the room – old windows set deep into thick walls are particularly effective. The shutters

Light reflecting off glazing bar

GLAZING BARS

Large, clear sheets of glass are not necessarily the most attractive windows. Traditional glazing bars (above and right) reflect light to create a luminous foreground screen that can brighten a room.

PROTECTIVE BLINDS

Delicate blinds over this expanse of glass provide an element of privacy while hardly affecting the view (above). They also offer control against excess sunlight.

A LIGHT CORNER

In this room, light reflects off the sides of the deep walls, the rooflights and the wide window seat – an inviting place to sit (right). Thin window frames emphasize the solidity of the masonry.

REFLECTED LIGHT
This small opening in a modern room emulates a traditional, deep-cheeked window (below). The sides reflect the light, making the opening seem larger while focusing on the view.

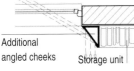

Additional angled cheeks   Storage unit

REFLECTING MAXIMUM LIGHT
Increase the cheeks either side of an opening so that the windows appear to be set in thick walls that reflect light into the room. This can be done by increasing the depth of the fittings or insulation (above).

surrounding windows of some period houses also reflect light, yet many people lose this effect by stripping the shutters back to the natural wood.

▶ Where deep walls are not available, the same effect can be created by making deep 'cheeks' to the windows. To do this, bring the sides of cupboards or bookcases – preferably with an angled surface – tight up around the window. The depth of the unit will extend the depth of window jamb.

▶On tall windows, add high-level window shelves that catch the light and reflect it onto the ceiling – this is particularly effective in deep rooms.

SIDE LIGHTING

The light entering these rooms would hardly be visible without the reflected patches of sun on the wide columns (left). This demonstrates the value of a sunlit surface, seen in the distance from a darker space.

NOTE
Do not replace walls with glass until you check whether they serve as fire separation or protection.

▶Take a tip from Scandinavian design traditions. Their interiors traditionally feature pale yellows, blues, turquoises and greys, all containing a good deal of white, which bounces the light across the surfaces and suffuses the rooms with a luminous quality. Shutters are used at night instead of heavy curtains, so that for daytime privacy only sheer, open weaves and muslins are needed. During the day, sheer fabrics at the windows catch whatever light is available and reflect or diffuse it to maximum effect.

▶ Light surfaces outside a window such as paving or balcony floors, walls and plants, play an important part in reflecting light into a room. A garden pool outside a window can throw considerable amounts of light into a room – light that is vibrant and alive as the water moves and casts ripples on walls and ceilings.

▶ Light-coloured foliage is also useful near a window. Ideally this should be deciduous, so that the branches are bare in winter and do not shade precious daylight from the room. Remember that in a room facing away from the sun, the view of something sunlit opposite can be nearly as good – paint a wall light or plant silver or golden foliage that will catch the sun.

OUTSIDE SURFACES

The sun reflected off this bright garden wall and the light green foliage outside makes a significant contribution to the brightness and atmosphere of the room.

VERNACULAR SCREENING
These decorative pierced screens create cool by protecting the interior from external heat (right).

LIGHT SCREENS AND FILTERS

▶ In hot countries, and on the sunniest days in colder climates, you may need to filter and modify the light that streams into your home. Look at the older building traditions of North Africa, Spain and Japan, where screens, blinds and shutters that catch and filter light cast attractive patterns.

▶ Screens and slatted blinds have visual as well as functional advantages, as they can be used for privacy and to modify light during the day – when you are working at a VDU monitor for example. When selecting a screen or blind, remember that the nearer you are to it, the more you see through it, while a person across the road will see considerably less. Effective screens can be created

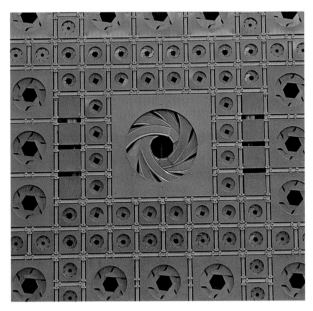

ARAB INSTITUTE, PARIS
In this building, a modern version of a traditional screen adjusts to let in more or less daylight according to external brightness (above).

Dark corridor

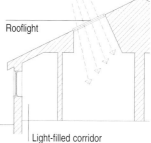

AFTER

Rooflight

Light-filled corridor

LATTICED SCREENS

Delicate wooden lattices create a sense of enclosure and privacy in this room and add a rich pattern to the large panes of glass (left).

STAINED GLASS

An unappealing view of a car park has been transformed into an ever-changing burst of colour by this specially commissioned stained glass, designed by artist Sarianne Durie (above).

without disturbing existing glazing by putting slats or even thin shelves across the insides of windows.

▶ Pierced lattice screens with attractive patterns were developed in subtropical cities such as New Orleans. European designs were elaborated in timber and iron, creating a richness similar to the vernacular traditions of Moorish and Persian architecture. The beauty of light-infused spaces created by the pierced marble screens and reflecting marble surfaces in the Islamic-Indian palaces at Fatehpur Sikri, Agra and Delhi and the exquisite pierced wooden shutters and screens in the Alhambra in southern Spain offer inspiration for dealing with excessive sun in similar but more modest ways.

▶ Stained glass can introduce light of rich, strong colours. It can be used in homes but is relatively expensive and will reduce light levels considerably. Where light is not essential to the use of a room, such as in a hall or on a landing, stained glass can create dramatic and attractive effects – for example a design that is predominantly yellow can give a sunny glow in north-facing spaces. (See p.191 for recommended reading on the use of stained glass in the home.)

PLANNING FOR LIGHT

Some of these principles were used in planning the alterations of an urban house (above). A first floor back extension had a bathroom with windows facing sideways, leaving a long dark internal corridor leading to the back room. By inverting the original arrangement and placing the bathroom on the inside wall, the corridor benefited from the windows while the bathroom was given a rooflight. The corridor is now a sunny space filled with books which acts as an extra room. The bathroom is flooded with light earlier in the day and needs no curtains for privacy.

ARTIFICIAL LIGHT

A RANGE OF LIGHTS

This carefully lit interior uses a range of energy-efficient lights to good effect. Low-voltage intense downlighters illuminate the picture, a compact fluorescent uplighter washes the wall with brightness and tungsten halogen lights create a pool of light over the dining table.

WHILE GOOD ARTIFICIAL ILLUMINATION IS ESSENTIAL IN the home, it consumes vast amounts of electricity. It is estimated that British households spend £1.2 billion a year on electricity for lighting – most still with inefficient tungsten lamps. Energy-efficient lamps – of which there are several different types – use as little as 20 per cent of the energy consumed by tungsten lamps. This reduces household energy bills and the amounts of carbon dioxide emission from electricity generation. In the UK, only two per cent of electricity is generated from renewable sources – more than 60 per cent comes from fossil fuel (oil, gas and coal) and almost 33 per cent is nuclear.

TUNGSTEN LAMPS

The earliest form of artificial lamp, tungsten lamps work in a similar way to candles. Electricity is used to burn a tungsten filament in argon gas, giving off heat as well as light. These lamps are extremely inefficient: no more than 15 per cent of the energy consumed is given out as light. The rest is heat. They last only about 1,000 hours because the metal filament burns away. Tungsten light has a yellow cast, similar to the glow of late afternoon sunlight, which is why tungsten light is thought to be warm. The light is directional, which gives modelling and highlights texture.

COMPACT FLUORESCENT LAMPS

Compact fluorescent lamps (CFLs) work by heating an inert gas contained within a glass tube. They are four to five times more efficient than tungsten lamps because once the gas has been energized, very little electricity is required to keep it glowing. The light emitted from an 11-watt fluorescent lamp, for example, is as bright as a 60-watt tungsten lamp. Because nothing burns, it gives off only a little heat and has a much longer life than tungsten – normally up to 10,000 hours.

Originally, fluorescent lights were made only in long tubes, but they are now universally available as compact fluorescent lamps, or CFLs, which can be installed in most

NOTE

Electricity is dangerous – it can cause lethal shocks and faulty or old wiring can start fires. Have your electricity installations checked when moving into a new home and have new installations carried out by a qualified electrician.

light fittings. Although CFLs are more expensive than tungsten lamps, the combination of lower electricity consumption and a longer life means that CFLs become more economic after the relatively short time of 1,500 to 2,000 hours (the life of two tungsten lamps).

CFL technology is improving all the time. The early problems that gave these lamps a bad name, such as their shorter life when used in low temperatures or when switched on and off frequently, and their slow start-up times, are being eliminated. Check these points with your retailer when buying lamps, however, as not all manufacturers have resolved the difficulties. CFLs pose no risk of fire, and fittings designed for them are made in many different materials, including recycled paper and wood.

The colour rendering of CFLs is very different from that of tungsten lights. The gas glows with colours high in the ultraviolet, blue and green ranges, which gives the light its cold, bluish appearance – the reason why many people still prefer to use tungsten. But developments in the technology now allow the glass tubes of CFL lamps to be coated, creating different colour renderings described as 'warm white', 'cool white' and 'daylight', or 'full-spectrum'. Daylight lamps are considered healthier as they more closely emulate the colour range of natural daylight.

The light from fluorescent lamps is also emitted over a large area, so it is more diffused and less directional than tungsten light. Older types of fluorescent lights oscillated at frequencies close to the brain's alpha waves and there were concerns that the flicker, even though invisible, was dangerous. Frequencies are now much higher and these concerns are no longer valid.

Compact fluorescent lights provide the same brightness as tungsten lamps with a lower wattage, thereby saving electricity. The following table compares the two:

Tungsten	CFLs
60 watts	11 watts
75 watts	18 watts
100 watts	20 watts

TUNGSTEN HALOGEN LAMPS

Low-voltage tungsten halogen lamps burn tungsten elements in halogen gas, making them more than twice as efficient as older tungsten fittings. The wattage can also generally be lower because all the light is concentrated on a smaller area, therefore increasing apparent brightness. Lower wattages also reduce electricity consumption. Tungsten halogen lamps are small, with a strong directional beam. They are available with beam angles ranging from 5 to 30 degrees and with warm and cool light characteristics, as well as in a range of strong colours. They have a life expectancy of 2,000 to 4,000 hours.

Because halogen lamps are low voltage they require a transformer which can be contained in the base of the fitting or located away from the lamp in a ceiling void or cupboard. Unlike other high-efficiency lamps, tungsten halogen fittings can be used with dimmers.

Low-voltage lamps contain mercury vapour and halogens. When their use becomes more general, disposal could become a problem, since the lamps could give off polluting emissions if not properly dealt with.

LIGHTING DESIGN

Lighting choices can make a radical difference to the appearance of the home, affecting the appearance of rooms and objects as well as the colour, texture, mood and atmosphere. The lowest possible energy consumption needs to be combined with the selection of the appropriate quality of light required – soft and diffused for general illumination, or brightly focused for tasks or display. This will govern your choice of lamp types.

There are also important safety considerations. Artificial lighting must meet a number of criteria: it must be safe for the task in hand – whether it is general illumination in corridors or stairs to avoid falls, or detailed task lighting for such activities as reading or sewing. If you spend a lot of time working in a room that needs artificial light during the day, it is healthier to use full-spectrum lights that emulate daylight. These lights have been shown to counteract some of the effects of low winter light levels, which cause Seasonal Affective Disorder, or SAD (see p.40).

Energy consumption can be drastically reduced by ensuring that lights are only switched on when needed.

SOFT LIGHTING

A focused downlighter provides an interesting pinpoint of light in this dim, cool interior. It augments the shaft of natural light from the double doors.

More and more installations are becoming 'intelligent' – the light comes on when they sense the presence of people, then goes off when not needed. Usually only used in public places, or for external safety lights, they could be helpful in areas of the home such as halls and passageways, where lights may otherwise be left burning all night.

TIPS

▶ Install as many low-energy lamps as possible.

▶ Design lighting for maximum task efficiency.

▶ Turn lights off when not needed.

▶ Use time switches or sensors on external lights so that they are not left burning all night.

HEAT

See more technical discussion on pages 172–89

INDOORS, OUR BODIES ARE GENERALLY COMFORTABLE IN a temperature range of 18–27°C. But most people (except those living in extreme climates) experience natural external temperatures ranging from below freezing to 38°C or more. The need to create a comfortable living temperature from such external extremes explains why home heating consumes so much fuel and energy. Vast amounts of the earth's natural and irreplaceable resources are expended on home heating, with environmental consequences that are endangering our health and future. Hence it is well worth thinking about how to minimize the heat input necessary to create the comfort we need.

The thermal performance of any home largely depends on its basic construction and orientation. Nevertheless, the homemaker can make a number of improvements that will significantly reduce fuel use and energy costs while creating a comfortable home.

▶ Turn down the heating in your home by a few degrees. You will save fuel and may feel better, too.

▶ Increase insulation to reduce energy demands.

▶ Seal your home so that as much energy as possible is retained, but make sure that it is also well ventilated (see pp.74–83).

▶ Make use of free heat from the sun. This will also make your home attractive and bright (see p.66).

▶ Control heat so you use it only where and when it is needed.

▶ Use the most efficient fuel, heat source and method of heat distribution available to you.

KEEPING OUT THE COLD

Internal space is protected from outside cold (or heat) by insulation, which works by trapping layers of still air so as to minimize heat transference. This air can be held in a void, or in the interstices of a lightweight airy material. The best insulators are those that contain the most air: of these, the safest are wood, wool, flax and shredded paper. Dense materials, such as stone, are the worse insulators.

A WARM HAVEN

The walls of this warm, safe room are lined with unfinished softwood boarding. The wood-burning stove has doors that can be closed and is set in a massive masonry structure that will store and radiate heat.

INCREASING INSULATION

Walls of logs have long been used to make warm homes in cold climates. And thin layers of wooden panelling added to cold stone walls have long been a method of increasing warmth, as have rugs, weavings and tapestries. For hundreds of years, these have kept traditional homes warm and provided the opportunity for endless decorative invention – from the great tapestries and oak panelling in medieval castles to the simpler wall hangings and boarding in more modest homes. (For more on wall linings see p.124–131.)

The effectiveness of wall hangings or panelling can be increased by adding an insulating backing. But don't pack the insulation material too tightly – always allow room for air movement to avoid problems with condensation.

Double glazing and the use of special insulating glass help prevent heat from escaping through windows (see p.140).

Curtains, too, provide insulation and, as with wall hangings, the thicker the material used the better. Sew weights into the hems so that the curtains stay in place and keep out draughts more efficiently. If you have radiators below your windows, keep curtains short so that they hang above the radiator, and fix a shelf above the radiator to deflect heat into the room.

Curtains can also be hung over doors to keep out draughts. Blinds with reflective foil backings or insulating layers help to limit cold radiation from windows at night. Internal shutters are another good method of insulating windows. New shutters that fit in shutter boxes to match traditional timber are costly. Just as efficient are simpler shutters that can be hinged in the window surround or that slide on runners across the window. Adding insulation to these will make them even more effective.

WALL HANGINGS

Traditional hangings around an old four-poster bed keep warmth in and cold draughts out (above). This idea can also be used to enclose areas of a room.

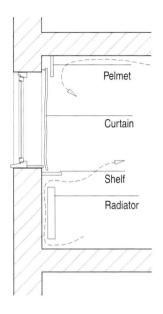

INCREASING EFFICIENCY

Two techniques for improving the efficiency of a radiator on an outside wall. A shelf over the radiator pushes the air out into the room. A pelmet above the window prevents the warm air circulating behind the curtains and on to the cold window.

Pelmet

Curtain

Shelf

Radiator

PREVENTING HEAT LOSS FROM FLOORS

Heat can also be lost through traditional raised ground floors which have air voids underneath. Air voids were developed as a healthy form of construction designed to keep timbers out of the damp earth and provide valuable ventilation to prevent or remove moulds and damp. For this reason, when insulating such floors to prevent heat loss into the air space, it is important to maintain through ventilation from one side of the house to another.

If the space under the floor is large enough to crawl into, you can staple or pin insulation to the underside of the floor structure. Use a semi-rigid or quilt insulation material, with a minimum thickness of 100 mm. If you cannot crawl under the floor, the only way to achieve good insulation is to lift the floorboards and drape netting over the floor beams (or joists) to contain the insulation.

DECORATIVE INSULATOR

Hung like a curtain over this large bedroom window, a beautiful kelim rug acts as an effective insulator and also makes a striking, decorative feature in the room (left).

INTERNAL SHUTTERS

Heat-retaining shutters on this bathroom window ensure that anyone using the bath is protected from cold draughts and has plenty of privacy (above). Wooden walls add warmth.

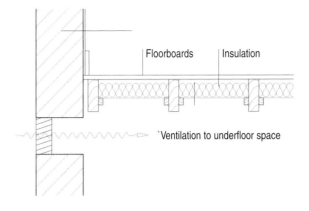

Floorboards Insulation

`Ventilation to underfloor space

RAISED GROUND FLOOR

Insulation materials placed between or under floor joists will increase the warmth of a raised ground floor (left). It is essential to keep the underfloor space well ventilated.

SOLAR GAIN

Large French doors allow plenty of sunlight to fall on to the dark, tiled floor of this room (right). The floor absorbs solar heat during the day and radiates it back into the room in the cool of the evening.

Alternatively, use a rigid insulation and rest this on battens fixed to each side of the joists. If you are unable to do such extensive work, the effect of draughty floorboards can be reduced with carpet and a thick underlay. Do not make the mistake of laying a plastic membrane under the floor in the hope that it will prevent damp – it will cause condensation. Dampness is best removed by ventilation.

Improve the insulation around your hot water tank by using a properly designed insulating jacket. Even better, replace an old tank with one that has an integral insulation. Ensure that loft spaces and other voids have the maximum amount of insulation – generally no less than 150 mm. Seek guidance from one of the many advisory organizations on home insulation – grants may be available.

SEALING IN WARMTH

Keep your home warm by minimizing the loss of warm air through draughts. There are two ways of doing this: first, seal gaps around doors and windows with rubber gaskets or nylon brush seals, and second, make lobbies at all the external doors. These can make attractive entrance areas that are also useful for storing coats and shoes or displaying houseplants. When sealing your home, make sure that you create adequate ventilation to keep the internal air healthy – see pp. 74–83 on ventilation. The ideal is a warm house that stays at a reasonably constant temperature and has adequate and controllable levels of ventilation – a principle that is described by the US Environment Protection Agency (EPA) as 'seal tight, ventilate right'.

COLLECTING THE SUN'S WARMTH

Heavy, preferably dark-coloured surfaces – concrete, tiles or stone – absorb the sun's heat through glass (solar gain) and radiate it back into the space when the temperature drops (right).

FREE HEAT FROM THE SUN – SOLAR GAIN

The sun is the greatest source of energy we have and it is free. While exploiting solar energy to the full requires comprehensive design of the building structure, significant benefit can be gained from relatively minor building work or specific decorating strategies. In most homes, the sun can provide up to about 10 per cent of warmth requirements, depending upon the building's orientation, setting and construction.

Anyone with a window that lets in direct sunlight knows how much heat can be generated through the glass – this is known as solar gain. The challenge is to capture and store this warmth for as long as possible after the sun has ceased to shine. Dark, heavy materials such as concrete, stone or tiles absorb and store heat, then radiate it back into the space when the outside temperature drops. To make best use of this in rooms with a sunny orientation, use materials such as slate, dark ceramic tiles or even dark, painted concrete on floors, worktops and other surfaces. The larger the area of glass, more southerly the orientation and the larger the absorbent surface, the greater will be

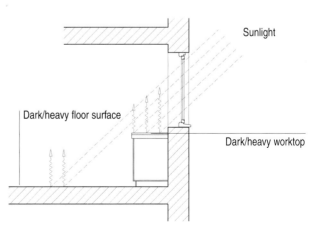

Sunlight

Dark/heavy floor surface

Dark/heavy worktop

Heavy stone walls and floors make efficient solar heat collectors in this sun-filled space (left). The massive stones store the sun's warmth.

A centrally placed wood-burning stove radiates heat into this whole studio area (right). It is an ideal form of heating in a large, high space.

the best possible use of the sun's warmth. The efficiency of your heating system will depend upon the following:

▶ Method of heat distribution
▶ Flexibility of controls
▶ Type of fuel and burner

Heat is transmitted in three ways: by radiation, convection and conduction. The first two play the greatest part in space heating. An ordinary central heating radiator illustrates the differences between these two forms of heat – the name 'radiator' is in fact a misnomer because radiators emit only 30 per cent of their heat by radiation and 70 per cent by convection.

RADIANT HEAT

Radiant heat is the most efficient method of transmitting heat because it heats only the areas on which it is focused – whether the body or objects around it. Convection, on the other hand, must warm the air before we feel any heat. The choice of which is most practical and effective will depend on the nature of the space and its pattern of use. In normal domestic rooms, where the whole space is used and occupants want to move freely, it is more comfortable to heat the whole space by convection. But in larger, high spaces, or those used intermittently, such as workshops, studios, occasional play rooms or stores, it is usually more efficient to use radiant heat that is focused on the area of activity, thus avoiding having to heat large volumes of air. Another advantage of radiant

the capacity to store and re-radiate heat. This idea must, of course, be balanced with the desire to have light surfaces near windows to reflect light and increase brightness (see pp.40–57). The choice is yours.

With some building work, it is possible to enlarge windows, add a bay or make a glazed-in porch, all of which collect solar gain. The larger the amount of external wall these devices can cover, the better, but bear in mind that any large glazed areas must be made of insulating glass. Many of the ideas discussed in the chapter on light can be developed to provide solar warmth. Solar panels, of course, are the most effective way of making use of solar gain and can substantially reduce energy costs. (For more information, see books listed on p.207, and sources on p.198)

EFFICIENT HEAT DISTRIBUTION

In most existing houses a heating system is needed at some times of year, even if we do increase insulation and make

RADIANT HEAT
Radiant heat is the most efficient form of heating because if gives it heat exactly where it is needed, immediately (left). It is ideal in rooms with high ceilings.

heat is that it is not lost through ventilation. However, some people may find the sensation of radiant heat from above uncomfortable.

The simplest radiant devices are electric bar heaters, but these are dangerous. Safer and more practical, with a larger heat spread, are flat panels, which are heated either by electrical elements or by water pipes mounted behind them so that they are relatively unobtrusive. The larger the panel, the greater the heat output.

One of the disadvantages of radiant panels is that they can be dangerously hot to touch, but new types are available that have a relatively low temperature (25–45°C) and can be inset flush with the wall if you remove the plaster. They come either as mats with electrical coils or as thin, pre-formed radiators. Some can even be fitted behind plaster or plasterboard so that they cannot be seen. These inset panels radiate a gentle warmth and keep the fabric of the wall warm. The dis-advantage is that if you go out of their range you will not benefit from any heat, so the ambient air temperature should not be too low.

CONVECTED HEAT

Convected heat has a number of health disadvantages: it dries body tissues and membranes in our eyes, nose, throat and skin, leading to irritations and making us susceptible to colds. This is one of the factors cited for winter cold syndromes. Convected air also stirs up dust, exacerbates odours and has a slower warm-up time.

Convection heaters work by heating air as it passes over hot surfaces. Thus, the larger the surface area, the larger

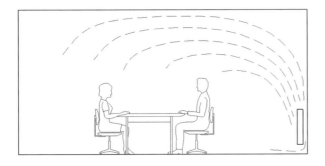

CONVECTED HEAT
Convected heat relies on air passing over a hot surface: a space will become warm only when the whole volume of air is heated.

the heat output. Fins on the back of a radiator increase the surface area without increasing its width or height. Also available are very compact radiators that are enclosed and contain a fan that draws air in from near the floor and forces it up over the hot fins. Known as 'convector heaters', these are small and efficient, but should generally be avoided because the fans consume electricity, stir up dust and require maintenance.

Whatever form of heating you choose, be sure to locate heat emitters carefully and consider the following points:

▶ Avoid placing radiators on outside walls, where some of the heat will radiate to the outside, unless precautions are taken.

▶ Distribute heat evenly by having more small radiators or heaters rather than a single large one.

INSULATION
This room, constructed from timber logs,
is well insulated and needs no other
adornment. The window is triple glazed.

most efficient, a thermostatic control. This allows the temperature in each space to be adjusted for individual comfort and pattern of use, and reflects weather conditions or indoor heat-generating activities such as cooking. For even greater efficiency, arrange any new installation so that areas of the house with different uses – such as bedrooms and living rooms – are on separate heating circuits, allowing them to operate at different times and levels of heat.

Remember, too, that our sense of comfort depends on the amount of ventilation available, the activity we are engaged in and our personal metabolism. The greater the amount of control we have over the heating in our homes, the more easily we can accommodate these factors and ensure minimum wastage and maximum comfort.

UNDER-FLOOR HEATING

Another way of heating efficiently is to keep the fabric of the home at a good background temperature. You can then top up the heat in individual rooms, depending upon weather conditions, and introduce high heat only where and when it is needed. This works particularly well in heavy masonry buildings which, if left unheated at night or for parts of the day, can become very cold and require large amounts of energy to bring them up to a reasonable temperature. A background heat of about 12–15° Centigrade will mean that on many days in the winter months only a small boost of extra heat is required to make the house comfortable. In cold climates, background heat is also important for protecting the building from frost and condensation damage.

Underfloor heating, preferably using hot-water pipes rather than electric cables, is an ideal form of background heating for homes with solid concrete floors covered with stone or tiles. Proprietary systems using hot water pipes with timber flooring are also available. Underfloor heating radiates a general background heat into the space and makes cold floors comfortable.

▶ Add spacer blocks behind radiators to increase the air movement.

▶ If a radiator has to be on an outside wall, place as much insulation behind it as possible and add a reflective membrane.

▶ Avoid obstructing heaters with furniture or curtains.

▶ Fit a shelf above any radiators under windows so that the air moves out into the room instead of rising behind curtains or blinds.

CONTROLLING HEAT

Flexibility of control can reduce energy consumption. The approach of simply letting a boiler run in the winter months, pumping heat into the whole dwelling is grossly inefficient and should be avoided. Heating can be operated by a simple on-off switch, a pre-set time clock or,

Although expensive to install, this form of heating is efficient for two reasons. First, it warms the feet, often the coldest part of the body, which allows the general room temperature to be a few degrees lower than normal. Second, the heavy mass of a solid floor allows heat input to be intermittent because the floor will store warmth and so remain at a relatively stable temperature. Pipes and cables need to be embedded in a sand and cement layer (screed) that is no less than 75 mm thick. If you do not have enough depth in the floor for cables or pipes, a system using thin mats containing slender cables is available. These will not provide full heating, but will simply take the chill of the stone.

WOOD-BURNING STOVES

Stoves make any home look warm and cosy and are an ideal way of boosting background heat. Wood is a renewable resource, but wood-burning stoves are only environmentally sound if they are efficient, high-temperature models, (called clean-burn or double-circulation burners) which prevent the emissions of smoke and particulates. Wood-burning stoves can use low-grade timber and woodland industry waste and thinnings as well as pellets of waste – if using the latter, ensure that their content is safe. Always burn dry wood – wet wood emits smoke.

Wood-burning stoves are also useful for providing that small amount of heat needed in spring and autumn, when external temperatures are beginning to cool, but heating the whole house is unwarranted. Greater efficiency can be achieved by linking a wood-burning stove with a back-boiler to one or two radiators in places that particularly need heating, such as the bathroom. In most temperate areas, a fire burning in a living area will give background heat that should shorten the period when central heating, is needed throughout the home. Dual instal-lations, where radiators can be served by either a central heating boiler or a backboiler, are ideal, but they can be expensive in capital terms and require careful design and sophisticated controls.

The heavier the stove – and particularly the more central and massive the chimney – the more efficient it will be because the structure as well as the stove will store and radiate heat into the house. This is the principle

behind the massive stoves used in northern Europe and Scandinavia.

When choosing a wood-burning stove, essential points to look for are:
▶ Closed-door type with a tight door seal
▶ Recirculating air chambers to maximize the burn-out of emissions
▶ Solid construction
▶ Ease of loading for safety

Ensure that any wood-burning stove is installed correctly by a qualified installer. Have your chimney swept at the end of every winter to avoid the risk of fires as a result of the build-up of tar in the chimney.

HEATING AND COOLING ENERGY AND RESOURCE USE

Homes consume a substantial proportion of national energy consumption: in the UK they account for some 27–30 per cent and in the USA some 38–40 per cent. While this book considers mainly how decoration, furnishings and fittings can contribute to a sustainable home, rather than construction work, every home will at some time require the replacement of its heating and hot water systems. These more than any other element of the home contribute to its sustainability. The last chapter – Home Energy Systems (pp.172–89) – discusses these systems and gives an overview of the issues and options available, and suggests priorities in terms of cost and benefit. This will allow an informed assessment about the most appropriate actions to take to make your home mores sustainable and which of the many options suit different homes in different circumstances. Whatever action you take, always bear in mind that 'less is more' – by far the most effective action, the cheapest, and which you should consider before any other, is to reduce your energy consumption.

AIR AND VENTILATION

LIKE SUNSHINE AND CLEAN WATER, FRESH AIR IS VITAL for healthy body processes, and access to it has been taken as a right. Today, we tend to forget its importance.

We need fresh air in our homes, not only for the body's metabolic functions but also to dissipate body bioeffluents. As in any process of transformation, the body emits waste. Those wastes that affect indoor air quality are water vapour, carbon monoxide and body odours. It is estimated, for example, that each person, when relatively static, emits about seven litres of water vapour per day into indoor air. Fresh air also removes mould spores and viruses from the home and prevents the accumulation of chemical offgassing, dust and uncombusted gases from appliances. In addition, air cools us when interiors become too warm.

The extent of the harmful effects of chemicals and dust on our indoor air quality is only just beginning to be understood. At present, statistics for health in workplaces are more readily available than those for health in homes. In a survey of 223 buildings, the occupants of which had complained of a variety of health problems, there was inadequate fresh air in 65 per cent and poor distribution of fresh air in 46 per cent.

Dust particles are one cause of poor indoor air: the problem is that the finer the particles, the less we are aware of them, but the more potential they have to harm our lungs. In addition, unventilated moist air encourages mould spores and bacterial growth – all of which affect our lungs and can potentially lead to respiratory diseases. When creating a healthy home, aim to eliminate the majority of pollutants at source by avoiding materials that offgas unwanted chemicals. But the need to replenish fresh air in the home regularly will always remain: the better the ventilation, the healthier the home.

CHANGING THE AIR

The amount of fresh air needed in any space for any given activity is expressed as the number of air changes per hour – this means the number of times the entire volume of air in a space is completely replaced with fresh air. The World Health Organization (WHO) recommends that in living areas, when people are generally static, perhaps carrying out quiet domestic tasks or relaxing, the air should be changed 0.5 times per hour – in other words, a complete air change every two hours. In an old, 'leaky' house, this need would be met automatically without any other actions. It has been estimated that loose-fitting windows, doors and open chimneys give an automatic background air-change rate in the order of 0.7 per hour. Recommended change rates for bedrooms are 1.3 times per hour, and for bathrooms, kitchens and any other areas where people are very active, they rise to 6 changes per hour. In rooms where people are smoking, as many as 10 to 15 air changes per hour are recommended.

Naturally occurring air-change rates have been radically reduced in modern, tightly sealed homes, making the need for proper ventilation even more pressing. Building regulations now require buildings to be sealed so that they are almost 'air-leak free' permitting only 0.1 air change per hour. This is one-fifteenth of the air change rates recommended by WHO.

CREATING PROPER VENTILATION

While outside air is often less clean than we might wish, it can still be up to ten times cleaner than indoor air. So, unless we suffer from sensitivities to particular external pollutants that need filtering out, it is best to ventilate with outside air rather than by using air conditioning. Air conditioners harm the environment by their energy consumption, the heat they emit into the atmosphere, and the use of polluting refrigerant gases. Simpler passive

A FLEXIBLE, TRADITIONAL DESIGN
This window arrangement offers flexibility and control (right). The under-sill panel is hinged so that it can act as a door in summer. Shutters provide deep, light-reflecting cheeks by day and insulation at night.

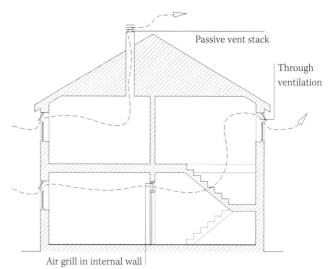

Passive vent stack

Through ventilation

Air grill in internal wall

PASSIVE VENTILATION

Openings positioned at high and low levels in a house allow the through passage of air and create natural (passive) air movement without the need for mechanical fans (right). Outlets at roof level are particularly effective.

techniques for ventilation and cooling have been used in vernacular buildings for centuries. These cost nothing, are safe to use, and have no environmental impact. A number of principles govern the movement of air in a building and it is useful to bear these in mind when looking at ventilation.

▶ Unequal air pressure exists on different sides of a building, which can create air flow.

▶ Air movement outside a building increases with height.

▶ Air inlet and exit positions are necessary for air movement.

▶ Warm air rises, while cold air falls – the 'stack effect'.

▶ Polluted air tends to rise.

▶ Evaporation cools a surface.

There are many ways to create good ventilation. Those most suitable for your home depend on factors such as the way it is built, its orientation and the size of the windows.

The best way to ensure a good air flow through a home is to have air inlet and exit positions (preferably at high levels) on different sides of the building, with clear routes for the air to travel between them. Except on the stillest days, the pressure difference on opposite sides of a building will draw air from one side through to the other. This applies to individual rooms no less than dwellings. It is much more efficient to have small openings on two opposite sides of a room than to have one window wide open.

Windows and skylights can be fitted with devices that allow a tiny opening to admit a trickle of air while avoiding a draught. There are two forms – one is a night-vent handle that keeps the window secure while it is slightly ajar. The other is a slot-ventilator that can be fitted into a window frame. This narrow channel has an open/closed

VENTILATION AND SHADE

A decorative window grill allows constant ventilation and provides shade. This simple room needs no other decorative features (left).

EXTERIOR SHUTTERS
Traditional shutters shield a room from the sun while allowing plenty of air movement (right).

slide position and provides a secure way of ventilating. It can be added to existing windows, either in the frame, provided it is thick enough, or at the top of the glass. Good-quality modern windows come ready fitted with night-vents or slot-ventilators.

AIRBRICKS AND SHUTTERS

Wall-mounted airbricks are an excellent way of creating natural ventilation. Unlike traditional airbricks, which are permanently open, these can be fitted with sliding or hinged covers for controlling the air flow. They can be located on external or inside walls to allow cross ventilation. In hot climates, large vent openings above doors or high up on walls can be used to allow plenty of air movement through a room, and these are not difficult to install. Another way of encouraging air circulation without loss of warmth is to install airbricks behind radiators, a technique that has been used in Scandinavia. This ensures that the incoming air is heated, rather than creating cold draughts. Controllable airbricks should be used in this situation.

Windows can be fitted with shutters, grills and trellises to allow ventilation while retaining privacy and security. Particularly effective and used in many European countries are shutters with hinged flaps so that it is possible to vary how much of the screen is open. In traditional buildings, screens and shutters are made in a wide variety of materials and patterns and can be attractive features. In Moorish Spain, for example, screens and shutters made of local timber were pierced with geometric shapes and patterns, illuminating the cool, dark interiors with pinpoints of light like the night sky. Moghul emperors adorned their palaces with heavy stone screens carved with elaborate patterns

INTERNAL SHUTTERS
Half shutters provide privacy while the window is open for ventilation (right). This allows light to stream in through the upper part of the window.

Open ventilation screens allow the movement of air that is cooled and moistened by the indoor pool (left) – a simple form of natural air conditioning.

A porch provides a cool, shady spot in which to enjoy the open air while sheltering from direct sunlight (right). The porch also shades the house walls from the hot sun.

that not only provided ventilation, but also absorbed the sun's heat (see p.54). These examples can still inspire us today to make passive yet efficient practical devices that are also decorative elements.

ROOF VENTILATORS AND VENT STACKS

Roof ventilators exploit the stack effect, releasing rising hot air. This is why old-fashioned chimneys were so effective at providing ventilation – and so draughty. Today, you can utilize the stack effect and create natural through-ventilation with high-level openings in rooflights, small flue-outlet pipes with ceiling grills, or airbricks placed high up on walls. Locate these openings in a central space, such as a stairwell or living room, and add small vents in the internal walls to interconnecting rooms. Air will be drawn in at low level and out at high level.

The principles of passive vent stacks have long been exploited in simple devices such as the wind scoops that are so common in the Middle East. With these as inspiration, a number of passive ventilation stack devices have been developed to ventilate internal rooms, particularly bathrooms, and to create natural ventilation throughout a home. They are essentially pipes that run vertically to vent at the top of a building, and rely on external air movement at high level to draw air up and out of the room. Specially shaped cowls assist the upward draw of air – the cowls can be fitted with small, low-energy fans to increase efficiency. In order to work properly, these devices require air coming into the house through any of the methods described above. Passive air inlet vents are available which respond to indoor humidity and open or close automatically.

YEMENI WINDCATCHERS

Traditional ventilation devices, these windcatchers at the tops of buildings in the Yemen have become attractive architectural features (left).

Passive ventilation systems are now accepted by building control authorities as alternatives to electric-fan extractors in bathrooms and kitchens. In the winter, it is more economic to have a continuous, slow-running small electric fan on a passive ventilation stack in a kitchen than to achieve the same ventilation by opening windows to let out large amounts of expensively heated air. Installation in a single storey or the upper floors of multistorey buildings is relatively easy, but the disruption involved in routing a system through two floors will depend on the layout of your home. It may be possible to take passive vent stacks through cupboards, but holes will have to be made in floors and ceilings. Avoid creating noise paths between rooms by wrapping the pipe in sound-reducing quilt. For more details, see pp.187–8.

COOLING

Air movement across the body causes the evaporation of moisture from the skin, which lowers body temperature. The greater the amount of ventilation (the faster the air movement) in a room, the cooler we remain. This is much easier in hot climates, where outside air brought into the building does not cause cold draughts. In cooler, more temperate climates, the problem is greater because we may want to cool down without losing expensively heated air, so a balance must be struck between air movement and heat loss.

Cooling by mechanical means can be achieved in two ways: fan-assisted air movement, which moves ambient air over the body, or air conditioning, which cools the air and then distributes it. If air flow is inadequate, fan-assisted air movement is much safer than air conditioning, which is environmentally damaging (see p.74). Ceiling fans can create comfort by assisting air movement but, because they consume electricity, should only be considered if passive ventilation techniques are not sufficient. While a fan obviously creates cooling air movement, its effectiveness in replenishing air depends largely on its position in relation to open windows.

A traditional method of cooling in hot climates combines the cooling characteristic of evaporation with the stack effect. Water is placed in a large porous jar at the base of a chimney or vertical vent stack. As hot air rises over the jar

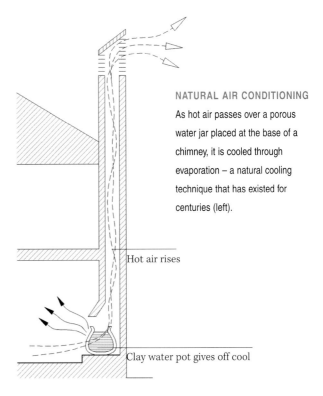

NATURAL AIR CONDITIONING
As hot air passes over a porous water jar placed at the base of a chimney, it is cooled through evaporation – a natural cooling technique that has existed for centuries (left).

Hot air rises

Clay water pot gives off cool

and up the chimney, it evaporates the water, lowering the temperature of both water and vessel. More air is then drawn into the chimney from below, constantly keeping air moving through the dwelling. This is effectively natural air conditioning. Even if you have no chimney, you can place a porous earthenware water container under an open window to gain something of this effect. The more porous the vessel, the better, as the surface of the jar itself has a cooling effect. An indoor pool or water feature is a more elaborate solution, which will not only cool the air but will also create a refreshing atmosphere.

BREATHING BUILDINGS

Another factor in determining healthy indoor air is the extent to which the construction of a building allows the dissipation of water vapour and bioeffluents. This is usually the case in older buildings made from natural vapour-permeable materials. Many modern building materials,

NATURAL VENTILATION
Whenever weather permits, throw windows open
to allow plenty of fresh air into rooms and stop the
build-up of stale air (below).

however, are impermeable and therefore seal in moisture-laden air, which contributes to damp and the growth of mould and spores which can cause respiratory problems. We see this effect regularly when warm, steamy bathroom or kitchen air condenses on tiled or gloss-painted walls. What we don't realize is that this process is taking place in all rooms of the house most of the time – even if walls are only partially permeable they tend to absorb much of the moisture that is generated.

Research into building construction, particularly in Germany and California, is showing that buildings are complex systems that react with people and the environment in a symbiotic, almost biological way. This theory, known as *bau-biologie*, demonstrates that buildings need to be constructed so as to breathe and be flexible and responsive to climate, air and moisture. Breathing buildings also help to create good indoor air quality.

As homemakers, we cannot change the construction of the buildings we live in, but we can help to make them more permeable and responsive by our decorating choices. Materials suitable for breathing walls are lime and mud plasters (normal gypsum plasters are partially permeable),

HIGH WINDOWS

In hot countries, rooms can be cooled by openings that maximize through-draughts. These high windows will let out rising hot air and generate cooling currents (left).

timber, cork and most fibreboards, fabrics, linoleum and low-fired, unglazed tiles. To summarize, the following guidelines will help you achieve healthy ventilation:

DO

▶ Ensure changes of air suited to the use of the room.

▶ Arrange ventilation openings such as windows and vents to assist through draughts.

▶ Fit night-vent handles or slot-ventilators on windows.

▶ Use passive rather than energy-consuming techniques.

▶ Install passive vent stacks.

▶ Use vapour-permeable paints and wall linings.

▶ On walls that require water-resistant materials, use linoleum, oily timber such as cedar, or tiles only on the areas that get wet.

DON'T

▶ Seal your home tight without ventilating it.

▶ Line walls with plastic materials.

▶ Use wall-sealing paints.

▶ Use an air-conditioning system.

VENTILATION FOR RADON GAS

Radon gas occurs naturally in the ground in some areas — usually where the underlying rock is granite. The gas rises and is dispersed, unless it becomes trapped in sealed areas beneath a building; then it can leak through the floor. However, radon has a short life when mixed with sufficient air. Protection measures, therefore, involve underfloor ventilation, which simply dilutes and disperses the gas. Full protection measures can only be achieved during construction, but in areas where radon is particularly high, partial measures to reduce its impact are recommended in existing buildings. These include installing continuously running fans to vent underfloor voids and wall cavities. This work should be carried out under the guidance of your local building inspectorate, who should have maps indicating areas where this problem exists.

SOUND

SOUND — WHETHER IT IS MUSIC OR NOISE — SURROUNDS us in a way that is more all-embracing than any other sensory stimulation. People often describe a sound as 'going right through you' and sounds have extraordinary emotive power. Unwanted sound — which is perhaps the best definition of noise — can affect us to such a degree as to cause stress and even illness. The power of sound may to some extent be due to the fact that sound is caused by the vibration of air waves, which resonate with our bodily vibrations. Noise increases the heart rate, while silence can slow it down and induce relaxation. A healthy home, therefore, needs to be a quiet home.

One reason why noise causes such significant levels of stress is because we can seldom control its source. We can turn away from things we don't want to see, or we can move to avoid touching something, but with noise, some-one, somewhere else, is in control. This stress-inducing factor adds to the simple physical damage to the ear caused by the prolonged exposure to noise.

The act of hearing involves two aspects of sound — the range of low to high sounds, referred to as frequency (measured as cycles per second) and the level of loudness (measured in decibels). Someone with good hearing will hear sounds from a low (bass) frequency of 20 cycles per second up to very high-frequency sounds of 20,000 cycles per second, regardless of whether the sound is loud or soft. This difference is important when dealing with noise because low-frequency sound is much more difficult to prevent than high-frequency sound. That is why, when noise comes through a wall, we hear many more low-level bass notes than the higher notes of speech or music.

COMFORTABLE ACOUSTICS

This room has comfortable, soft acoustics because the enclosing surfaces are not all parallel, so reducing the noise bouncing back and forth. The textured floor and ceiling also absorb and deaden internal noise.

SOUND, HEARING AND DANGEROUS NOISE

The relationship between our ability to hear a sound and its loudness level (regardless of whether it is high or low frequency) is not constant: each one decibel increase in measured sound levels reflects an increase in the intensity (or power) of sound by a factor of ten. Putting this simply, someone listening to the faint sound of a single bird singing in a quiet environment will be listening to a sound that would measure close to 0 decibels, which is considered the lowest threshold of hearing. A person with poor hearing who cannot hear sound below 40 decibels but wants to hear birdsong will need to listen not to 40 birds but to 10,000 birds, and someone who cannot hear below 50 decibels will need to be sung to by 100,000 birds!

To give an idea of what these sound levels mean in everyday terms, a quiet country area will have a background noise level of 20 to 30 decibels; a residential side road during the day might measure 45 decibels; a reasonably quiet office with quiet conversation will have a background level of 60 decibels, while busy offices can be in the order of 70 to 80 decibels. Noisy power tools and heavy traffic measure 80 to 100 decibels, while a loud rock concert measured within 15 metres of the speakers might be as much as 110 to 120 decibels.

Damage to hearing is caused by both the level of sound and the length of exposure. Recommendations for safe sound levels therefore specify both loudness level and period of exposure. Background noise of up to about 60 decibels should cause no disturbance, while 80 decibels is considered the maximum that is safe for any extended length of time. Exposure limits are recommended to be eight hours for levels up 85 decibels, two hours for up to 95 decibels and only 15 minutes for anything around 110 decibels. Above this, there is rapid hearing loss. The idea that hearing loss caused by noise is only temporary is a myth. Excessive noise exposure damages sensory cells in the ear that do not regenerate or repair. Unlike many illnesses, hearing loss is not reversible.

WAYS THAT NOISE IS TRANSMITTED

There are two types of sound – airborne sound and impact, or structure-borne, sound. Airborne sound is any sound that travels to the ear through the air – typically this includes speech, most music and traffic noise. Sound travels through the air in waves and the only satisfactory way of reducing the transmission of airborne sound is to block all paths through which sound waves travel.

Impact sound is generated by the impact of something heavy striking a surface, causing the sound to travel along or through the material. Footsteps on the floor of the room above or a neighbour banging on a party wall are typical impact sounds. Buildings with concrete floors or frames are much more susceptible to transmitting impact noise because the structure is continuous and sound can travel through the structure. For example, when pipes at one end of a building are hammered, the sound travels to the other end.

For an acoustically healthy home, there are a number of actions that can be taken:

▶ Reduce both airborne and impact noise coming into the home.
▶ Create a comfortable acoustic environment.
▶ Plan your home to reduce internal noise.

REDUCING AIRBORNE NOISE

Noise travels through the weakest link in any structure. So the sound reduction afforded by a heavy wall counts for little if a window is left open. When planning to reduce noise, we need to look not only at the mass of the wall, but also at the design of potential noise paths, such as windows, doors and any holes through walls for pipes or chimneys. Simple ways of limiting the amount of noise coming into your home include:

▶ Seal all noise paths or make them as tortuous for soundwaves as possible.
▶ Hang heavy curtains at your windows or consider fitting wooden shutters.
▶ Outside your home, add soft landscaping, which reduces the amount of sound reflected up into windows. Physical barriers, such as walls, fences and earth mounding, reflect traffic noise upwards and away from lower windows and garden areas.
▶ Add double glazing or, better still, secondary windows. Sound is attenuated by the size of the air gap between the panes of glass, so the larger the gap, the better the sound reduction. Line the reveals between the inner

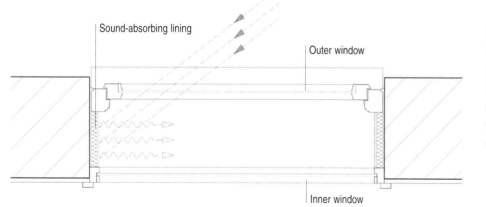

Sound-absorbing lining

Outer window

Inner window

DOUBLE WINDOWS

Sound insulation is best created by means of an air space between inner and outer windows (left). The sill, jambs and head between the windows should be lined with sound-absorbing material.

and outer panes in order to absorb some of the sound before it is transmitted through the inner pane.

NOISE REDUCTION WITH GLASS AND WINDOWS

Constant traffic noise can be a serious and debilitating problem, causing stress and sleep deprivation. The table below shows the typical levels of traffic noise from different sorts of roads and the reduction required to make comfortable sound conditions in living rooms and bedrooms. It also shows ways of achieving these reductions by the use

of different types of glass and windows. Figures are given in DBA – a measurement of noise disturbance rather than pure sound levels.

The noise-reduction measures that are outlined in the table might be costly. If you suffer from excessive traffic noise, consult your local environmental health officer, who will offer advice – and possibly even a grant towards costs. A glass manufacturer will also be able to help you. (For more information on different types of glass, such as laminated and audio-reducing, see pp.140–3.)

REDUCTIONS IN NOISE LEVELS (DBA) ACHIEVED BY DIFFERENT TYPES OF GLAZING

TRAFFIC NOISE MEASURED IN DBA*	LIVING ROOM RECOMMENDED LEVEL 40-45 DBA*	BEDROOM RECOMMENDED LEVEL 30-40 DBA*
RESIDENTIAL ROAD **60 DBA**	**20–15 REDUCTION IN DBA** USING SINGLE GLAZING 6 mm float (ordinary glass)	**30–20 REDUCTION IN DBA** USING SINGLE GLAZING 6.4 mm laminated glass
MAJOR ROAD **70 DBA**	**30–25 REDUCTION IN DBA** USING SINGLE GLAZING 7 mm audio-reducing glass	**40–30 REDUCTION IN DBA** USING DOUBLE GLAZING 13 mm and 13 mm audio-reducing glass
CITY CENTRE **75 DBA**	**35–30 REDUCTION IN DBA** USING DOUBLE GLAZING 7 mm audio-reducing glass and 10 mm float	**45–35 REDUCTION IN DBA** USING DOUBLE WINDOWS 6 mm float, 100 mm space, 4 mm float
MOTORWAY **80 DBA**	**40–35 REDUCTION IN DBA** USING DOUBLE WINDOWS 6 mm float, 150 mm space, 4 mm float	**50–40 REDUCTION IN DBA** USING DOUBLE WINDOWS 10 mm float, 200 mm space, 6 mm float

NOISE LEVELS

This chart shows the noise levels produced by different traffic situations. It also shows how to achieve the necessary reductions in noise to achieve comfortable sound levels in living rooms and bedrooms. DBA is a measurement of sound that relates to human comfort and is used for specifying noise disturbance levels.

NOISE REDUCTION THROUGH WALLS

The best way to prevent transference of noise through walls is to make the walls heavier by, for example, adding layers of plasterboard, heavy plywood or ceramic tiles. The lower the frequency of the noise, the heavier the wall has to be if it is to have any effect in reducing it. Adding sound-absorbent materials also helps, particularly with higher-frequency sounds such as high-pitched music, the upper levels of speech and children's voices.

As an architect, I dealt successfully with the problem of noise coming through walls in a nineteenth-century terraced house. The occupants were suffering as a result of loud noise coming through the party wall from next door and all their appeals for peace were ignored. The solution was a combination of mass and absorption. The wall was lined with four layers of 12.5 mm plasterboard, which was fixed to battens. The space between the battens was filled with sound-insulating quilt, which is much denser than heat-insulating quilt. To ensure that the installation covered all the potential weak spots, including voids in the ceiling and floor structure, we lifted floorboards and cut into the ceiling so that the new lining extended into and across all of these voids.

I had warned the client that it would be impossible to predict the extent of sound reduction because sound through structures, particularly when they are old, relies on so many factors. After the alterations, there were still occasional low-frequency rumbles, but the noises were so much fainter and less frequent that the family was relieved of sound-induced stress.

It is also possible to increase the mass of a floor in a number of ways, most commonly by adding some sound-insulating quilt or sand within the structure. Different types of sound-reducing mats and underlays are available from builders' merchants and are are particularly effective for reducing impact noise.

> ## NOTE
> If planning to increase the load on any structure by adding mass, first check with a structural engineer or your local authority building inspector that the existing structure is sufficiently strong for the extra load.

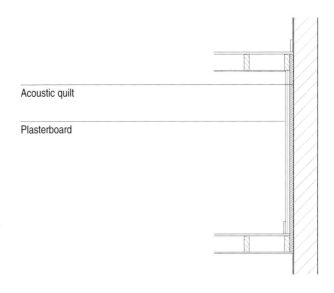

Acoustic quilt

Plasterboard

INCREASING SOUND REDUCTION

To improve the sound-reducing performance of a wall , add plasterboard to increase weight and stop low-frequency noise, and acoustic quilt to absorb high-frequency sound (above).

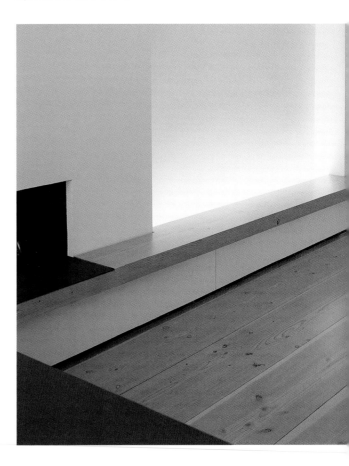

HARSH ACOUSTICS

The smooth, hard surfaces and lack of soft furnishings in this sophisticated minimalist dining room will create harsh, echoey acoustics (left).

SOFT ACOUSTICS

The wooden ceiling and textured surfaces in this room are excellent sound absorbers (above). The low-energy lights bounced off the wood give a warm glow.

REDUCING IMPACT NOISE

A hard surface transmits noise by acting like a drum. So to prevent noise transmission, the source of the impact noise must be isolated from the underlying structure. For example, a washing machine mounted on an absorbent surface transmits far less noise than one placed on a hard surface. Avoid acoustically absorbent materials made of foamed plastics and use cork, rubber or felt instead. Carpet is also a useful sound-absorber, but it will tend to depress over time and lose its value. Special anti-vibration mounting blocks can be obtained for machinery such as boiler pumps.

Kitchens and bathroom walls can generate noise because of the many hard surfaces they contain. Be aware of this when locating a sink, WC, or water tanks or pipes, bearing in mind that the vibrations of running water will transmit noise into an adjacent room. If such fittings must

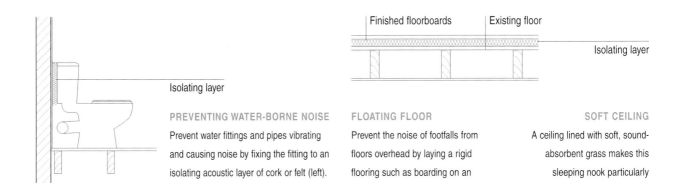

PREVENTING WATER-BORNE NOISE
Prevent water fittings and pipes vibrating and causing noise by fixing the fitting to an isolating acoustic layer of cork or felt (left).

FLOATING FLOOR
Prevent the noise of footfalls from floors overhead by laying a rigid flooring such as boarding on an isolating layer such as cork (above).

SOFT CEILING
A ceiling lined with soft, sound-absorbent grass makes this sleeping nook particularly cosy and quiet (right).

be located against an internal wall, they can be isolated with a resilient layer of cork or rubber. Or if you are putting tiling behind a sink, isolate the tiles by gluing plywood and a soft separating layer to the wall, then fixing the tiles or waterproof splashback to the board. The board must be glued – screw fixings create direct paths for sound transmission.

Noise in pipes can often be prevented by minor changes to the pipework installation. These need to be carried out by a plumber, who will suggest solutions to what could be a variety of problems, such as water hammer, restricted pipes or air locks. Noise transmitted by pipes commonly occurs when they pass through holes that are too tight – thereby transmitting the vibrations into the structure. Such holes should be eased and sealed with a flexible caulking compound.

An all too common problem is noise transmitted from the floor of one apartment to the rooms below. Airborne noise might be dealt with by making the ceiling heavier, but the real difficulties come if the apartment above yours has hard floors. The best solution is for your neighbours upstairs to install a resilient layer, such as carpet with good quality underlay. In bathrooms or kitchens where carpet is not practical, linoleum or rubber flooring can be laid over a thin resilient underlay for a similar effect. Resilient-backed sheet tends to be vinyl, so if installing such a floor, seek out the few products that are made with low petro-chemical or volatile organic compound (VOC) content.

A more complex and expensive solution is to install a 'floating floor', which isolates a hard wooden floor from the main floor structure by a continuous resilient layer. Doors and fittings will also need adjusting.

CREATING ACOUSTIC COMFORT

It is impossible to avoid sound being generated within the home, but whether or not this causes disturbance is dependent upon the acoustic quality of a space.

Hard surfaces such as stone, tiles, polished wood and plain plastered walls reflect noise and can create a very harsh acoustic environment. The extent of any problems will depend on individual noise tolerance and hearing as well as the use to which the space is put. An empty room with many hard surfaces may be fine when occupied by a couple talking, but if that space is filled with people and loud music, a very different and uncomfortable sound atmosphere may be created. This is because sounds are bounced off hard surfaces in all directions at the same time, sending the ear a mass of random mixed sounds. The same situation in a room full of soft furnishings will be far less disturbing, even though the level of sound generated may be much the same.

As sound is reflected from all surfaces in a room, it is not particularly important where you locate hard and soft surfaces. If you want to retain a beautiful polished timber or stone floor, compensate by adding full-length curtains and lots of soft furniture and cushions. Alternatively, try putting up some wall hangings or even something soft on the ceiling to absorb some of the sound

If you have a minimalist interior that is free from soft furnishings, but you want a more comfortable acoustic environment, you can install walls or ceilings with a backing of acoustically absorbent material, similar to that used in concert halls. The wall or ceiling is pierced, allowing sound to travel through to the soft backing, which absorbs the sound and prevents reverberation.

LOWERED CEILING

In this room, a lowered ceiling, consisting of textured, sound-absorbing panels, counteracts the resonant qualities of the hard floor and walls (left).

WALL OF WARDROBES

A wall lined with storage units makes a highly effective acoustic barrier to sound coming from neighbouring rooms or buildings (below).

PLANNING TO AVOID NOISE

If you can, minimize noise disturbance within the home by arranging the spaces so that noisy and quiet areas do not impinge on one another. For example, avoid situating play-rooms or TV rooms immediately adjacent to bedrooms. If your home offers no flexibility, consider using built-in furniture as a noise buffer. Line a wall between rooms that need sound separation with wardrobes. The more solid they are, the better, and they should cover the whole wall. Ideally, install a false back and line the space between the back of the wardrobe and the wall with acoustic quilt. If you want to listen to loud music or practise playing an instrument without disturbing other people, line the walls of your room with additional plasterboard to increase the mass. Consider installing a second door as is done in music practice rooms.

The smallest air path can render soundproofing efforts worthless. Tight air seals using rubber gaskets or cork are effective, but do remember to make sure that such rooms are well ventilated. Many of the solutions to airborne noise are similar to those for sealing warmth into buildings (see pp.62–73). They can serve both purposes (provided ventilation is addressed) since both heat and sound are transmitted, in part, through air paths.

PLANTS

THE FLOWERS, LEAVES AND SUPPLE FORMS OF PLANTS have long been an inspiration for decorators, painters, carpet weavers and architects. But the importance of plants for humans goes far beyond aesthetic enjoyment – plants are the mechanisms that transform the sun's energy into life. Only an urbanized society – one dissociated from the landscape – would ever need to remind itself of the importance of plants by conducting experiments to show that our heartbeats slow when we look at vegetation. Plants in the home can create some of the magic of gardens and, in sufficient numbers, they can soften the acoustic of a room. Even more important, plants can contribute to healthy indoor air quality.

Plants are always at work: via the process of photosynthesis, they convert sunlight into energy, giving off oxygen and absorbing carbon dioxide. They also transpire through their leaves and roots and help to modify humidity in the surrounding air. The foliage, roots and soil create a microclimate around the plant, which has a measurable effect on the space it occupies.

Pioneering research by Dr B. Wolverton at NASA, supported by research in Sydney, has shown that plants can process and absorb many of the unhealthy substances found in homes that contribute to poor indoor air quality and can cause illness. These include formaldehyde, VOCs (volatile organic compounds), xylene and ammonia. Plants also reduce airborne bacteria and fungi, and citrus plants appear to be able to sterilize air. Allowing the air to reach all parts of the plant, including its soil and micro-organisms, contributes to this process. The larger the leaf area, the better, so plants with many smaller leaves can be just as effective as large-leafed plants.

HOME FOR PLANTS

An ideal living room, this large, light, plant-filled area is only partly glazed to balance solar gain with the potential loss of heat in winter

DRAMATIC FEATURE

A single plant provides a striking
visual element in this classic setting
and also helps to clean the air (left).

The research suggests that certain plants have an effect on particular chemicals found in the home. If you are unsure about the chemicals you need to deal with, choose plants that are effective against a range of the more common household emissions. The spider plant, bamboos, rubber plant, peace lily, areca palm, and English ivy, for example, appear to be effective against formaldehyde, carbon monoxide, benzene and xylene. Another study has shown that plants reduce the amount of particulates in indoor air – particulates seem to adhere to plant surfaces.

Plants also give off moisture into the air, so increasing indoor humidity. In winter, air is naturally dry and is made even drier by most heating systems, contributing to a range of allergic and respiratory disorders. Plants help to counteract this and bring humidity up to healthy levels of 40 to 60 per cent. Too much humidity, however, allows the growth of moulds and biological contaminants.

PLACING PLANTS

Although research on the beneficial effects of plants is relatively limited as yet, the evidence is sufficiently strong to recommend them as an integral part of any safe home, rather than simply decorative items. As a general rule, one plant should be allowed for every 10 square metres of floor space, assuming average ceiling heights of 2.3 to 2.6 metres. This means that you need two or three plants to contribute to good air quality in the average domestic living room of about 20 to 25 square metres.

Although many plants like light, they do not all have to be placed near windows. Many indoor plants originated in the dense shade of tropical forests and have a high photosynthetic rate. These can be placed in darker corners and are ideal for the home. When positioning plants, try to

GROUPING PLANTS

Plants thrive in groups, as in this room,
where they are placed next to a tree
trunk used as an architectural feature.

FLOWERS

Cut flowers may not remove toxins
and fumes, but they do help to
make a room look fresh and bright.

strike a balance between light and ventilation, because the effect of plants on indoor air pollution appears to be reduced if they are set in a draught. Think about the type of plant as well as the temperature and use pattern of a room. Trial and error is sometimes the only way to decide which plant will survive where. Place plants close to areas where you may spend long periods of time, such as desks and computer workstations where they will help to mop up harmful emissions.

Dr Wolverton's research has shown the following plants to be the most effective all-rounders in counteracting off-gassed chemicals and contributing to balanced internal humidity. Most are easy to maintain.

▶ Areca palm (*Chrysalidocarpus lutescens*)
▶ Bamboo palm (*Chamaedorea seifrizii*)
▶ Dwarf date palm (*Phoenix roebelenii*)
▶ Boston fern (*Nephrolepis exaltata bostoniensis*)
▶ Dracaena 'Janet Craig' (*Dracaena deremensis* 'Janet Craig')
▶ English ivy (*Hedera helix*)
▶ Kimberley queen (*Nephrolepis obliterata*)
▶ Peace lily (*Spathiphyllum wallisii*)
▶ Rubber plant (*Ficus robusta*)
▶ Weeping fig (*Ficus benjamina*)
▶ Spider plant (*Chlorophytum comosum variegatum*)

AIR CLEANERS

Ivy plants (above) and the peace lily (above left) are both highly effective at removing toxins from indoor air.

HEALTHY AIR

Two or three plants such as Dracaena (right) are enough to ensure healthy air in a room.

SCENT

SMELL IS PERHAPS ONE OF THE MOST SENSITIVE OF OUR sensory tools, yet more often than not it is ignored when selecting materials and furnishings. But when something is seriously amiss in the home – whether from a burning pan that could lead to a fire, a broken drain that could cause ill health, or escaping gas that might lead to an explosion – our noses often give the first warning of possible danger. These warnings should not be ignored – our sense of smell is designed to let us know when we are breathing unsatisfactory air.

All too often, though, our sense of smell is dulled through constant exposure to petrol and other environmental fumes, stale indoor air, or offgassing from carpets, paint and adhesives. We may think a smell has lessened over time, but we may simply have become accustomed to it, while the smell – and so the potential health hazard – is still as strong as ever.

Harmful smells emanate from a range of substances within materials, either because the chemicals contained in them are not stable, or through abrasion and degradation from wear, water, light and aging. Offgassing and biological contaminants – such as damp and spores from mould – are only detectable by smell, so your nose is your best sensing device for these problems. When selecting materials, think about their smell as well as their look and feel. Sniff a sample of synthetic carpet and then a piece of organic, chemical-free flooring and you will immediately notice the difference. Your personal safety is worth the few strange looks that you might attract when smelling a material or object in a shop.

SCENTING THE AIR
The scent from a huge display of spring flowers and blossom fills this room and sweetens the air. The flowers are perfectly positioned in front of the large window, where the warmth of the sun's rays helps to release their delicate fragrance.

SCENTED WOOD
Natural materials such as wood add
their own fresh, sweet smell to the
home. In this kitchen, the air is
further scented by bunches of herbs
hung up from the ceiling to dry.

REMOVING BAD SMELLS

If a material used in your home smells unpleasant, it may be unsafe. If possible, remove the source of the smell and introduce fresh air. If you cannot remove the item causing the offending smell, you could install a filter device. These contain either charcoal (activated carbon), which is good for removing smells from solvents, fuels and alcohol as well as body and cooking odours, or a mineral called zeolite, which is most effective for ammonia and urine smells from pets. Both work by a process of adsorption – the gaseous molecules adhere to the porous materials – but the filter materials become ineffective when in damp conditions. Filters will not remove formaldehyde, sulphur or nitrogen oxides, so they should not be seen as an alternative to removing unhealthy substances.

A traditional – and gentler – way of eliminating odours such as cigarette smoke is to burn candles. Apples also absorb odours but are only effective in small spaces. Avoid spray deodorizers – most of these do not remove the offending smell but simply mask it by injecting scented substances into the air.

A FRAGRANT HOME

Conversely, we know how welcome certain smells can be – sea air, scents of the open countryside, fragrant flowers. The contribution of these scents to a healthy home is as important as those made by silence or light. So integral to our health is the sense of smell, that a system of healing called aromatherapy combines the beneficial powers of fragrant essential oils with massage to improve health and well-being. In the home, these essential oils can be used in vaporizers to scent the air. A few drops of oil are added to water in a small ceramic or earthenware container and heated by a nightlight. As the oil warms, its scent wafts out into the room. Try lavender in the bedroom to encourage a good night's sleep or sandalwood to create a relaxing

atmosphere in a living room. Oils can also be added to candles, polishes and potpourri.

Other ways of making your home fragrant include placing vases of sweet-smelling flowers or bunches of aromatic herbs in every room. Herb sachets can be tucked into drawers and cupboards. Natural cedar blocks are an effective way of discouraging clothes moths – humans like the odour but moths don't.

Smell has undeniable power to activate the imagination and trigger memories and atmospheres. Everyone loves the aroma of freshly ground coffee and the smell of baking bread can take you back to your mother's kitchen. One of the many advantages of selecting natural materials for the home is that they smell good – rush and grass floors, timbers such as cedar and pine, and natural vegetable-based oils and wax treatments on wood and other surfaces all have their own delightful, evocative fragrance.

Ways of keeping your home healthy and fragrant include the following:

▶ Remove any materials that smell of chemicals or give off strong vapours.

▶ Switch off any combustion appliance at the slightest hint of gas or smell and have it checked.

▶ Arrange lots of free air movement if you have to work with strong chemicals.

▶ Ensure proper ventilation in all rooms, particularly bathrooms and kitchens, to avoid build-up of smells.

▶ Always ventilate enclosed spaces such as cupboards under the stairs or cellars – particularly if they are prone to damp.

▶ Don't use deodorizer sprays.

▶ Make your home fragrant with fresh flowers, herbs and essential oils instead of chemicals.

NOTE

Never, under any circumstances, ignore the smell of burning or smells that emanate from gas appliances – they can kill.

ELECTRICITY

THE USE OF ELECTRICITY, AS MUCH AS ANYTHING else, distinguishes homes today from those of the pre-industrial past. Electricity makes our lives infinitely easier, but it also poses problems for our planet and electric fields may damage our health. Whether or not health dangers exist is debated at the highest scientific levels. All I can hope to do is to identify some of the issues that many people consider threatening to health in the home and suggest precautionary actions that may minimize risks.

X-rays, microwaves and other special and powerful electrical fields are universally accepted as dangerous. It is the weaker electric fields encountered everywhere in daily life that cause continuing disagreement among scientists. Two factors make it difficult to form a definitive view: first, low-level electric and electromagnetic fields are invisible; second, any effect on our bodies arises from a slow build-up over time. This build-up may not cause any apparent damage to most of us, but if it becomes sufficiently great, or if the immune system is already weak, the effects may overcome the body's natural tolerance and spill over, causing noticeable symptoms.

With the proliferation of electrical equipment – computer screens, mobile phones and wi-fi – our exposure to electric and electromagnetic fields other than those that occur naturally, is increasing all the time. Illnesses linked to electrical stress range from headaches, low-level fatigue, disturbed sleep patterns and inability to concentrate, to chronic fatigue syndrome, epilepsy, multiple sclerosis, disturbances of the nervous system and cardiovascular problems. Some of these illnesses have grown exponentially in the last 50 years and are part of the significant growth in immune-deficiency diseases for which no one has yet conclusively proved a cause. It is significant that the advice from the US government is to avoid risks until more is known about this subject. The relatively recent introduction of powerful yet invisible electromagnetic technologies into our lives means that we are, in effect, part of an experiment, the outcome of which we are unlikely to know for generations. Sceptics should remember that when X-rays were discovered, no one gave any thought to their dangers – today these are universally acknowledged.

ELECTRICITY AND OUR BODIES

Electricity is created by the vibration of energy. It has long been known that molecules vibrate when they absorb or emit electromagnetic fields. Many of the processes that take place inside our bodies, particularly those linked to neurological activity, operate through extremely low-frequency electrical charges. Since mains electricity is so much more powerful, it does not seem unlikely that it should cause disturbances to the small but vital electrical charges in our bodies.

Electricity produces two fields of force that can affect us: electric fields and electromagnetic fields. Their impact on us is determined by their strength and by the length of time we are exposed to them. Electricity, rather like water in a pipe, remains active in cables all the time, so even when we are not using light or power, electric fields are present in buildings. Like ripples in a pond, electric fields become weaker as distance from the source increases, and they are absorbed by any materials that conduct electricity – metal objects, walls and even people. Protection from the effect of fields is therefore relatively easy to achieve by increasing our distance and creating physical separation. The Swedish government, who do recognize that there may be risks, advise keeping one metre away from any field-generating equipment. So, for example, try not to put your kitchen table next to the fridge or microwave, or your bed near a night-storage heater or a fusebox.

Electromagnetic fields are more problematic because, while their effects fall off with distance, few materials

HEALTHY HAVEN
The absence of electrical equipment and other clutter makes this bedroom a peaceful – and healthy – haven.

exist that offer any protection. The fields pass through most building materials (except lead), and through people and the ground. The problem is compounded because much of the equipment generating these fields is used at close quarters – computer screens, televisions, microwaves, mobile phones. The only way to avoid potential danger is to keep your distance from such equipment when possible and to minimize the length of time that it is used.

ELECTRICAL STRESS IN THE HOME

Electrical stress in rooms where we remain in one place for a long period, such as the bedroom, is likely to pose the greatest dangers. In many bedrooms there is a concentration of electrical appliances beside the bed, near the sleeper's head – just where the electrical activity in the body is most intense. Normally, two or more power points supply electricity to appliances such as lights, radio, clock, baby alarm and telephone. In addition, there may be a television nearby, with a remote control at the bedside. Electric blankets are the worst offenders of all because they effectively wrap the body with electrical fields. Electrical interference with patterns of sleep is thought to affect the essential restorative function of sleep, which is considered to be the result of electrical activity in the brain.

A device called a demand switch allows you to switch off the electric current in the bedroom at night. The switch can be fitted to individual circuits on the mains panel. The circuits supply a small but continuous, safe, direct current to the circuit and cut off the electricity when not in use until you activate the appliance. Before fitting a demand switch, seek the advice of a specialist, as you will need to maintain electricity supplies at night to run boilers, time clocks, water heaters, refrigerators and freezers.

TVS, REMOTE CONTROLS AND COMPUTERS

These generate high levels of electromagnetic fields, but if we don't stay too close for too long, they should pose few problems. The general advice is to stay at least one metre from the set when watching television. Avoid keeping a remote control close to you for long periods. The use of television remote control devices also results in a waste of energy. Because the set remains in the 'on' or 'standby' mode even when switched 'off' by the remote, it uses almost as much electrical current as when fully functioning. This waste of energy is so great that the UK government is considering legislation to prevent television manufacturers producing sets with this facility.

Electromagnetic fields emanating from computer screens and from wi-fi routers are also a potential danger, although the increasing use of flat-screen technology, which operates without electromagnets, may soon reduce this hazard. Sweden first introduced safety standards after studies on animals found evidence of the adverse effects caused by exposure to radiation from monitors. Studies in the USA and Canada on pregnant women have given similar findings. The evidence is not yet conclusive, but there is sufficient to urge caution. Most radiation comes from the sides and rear of a screen, so the proximity of anyone else in the room should be considered.

KITCHEN APPLIANCES

A normal electric oven has a significant electric field that becomes negligible at a distance of about one metre. Other kitchen appliances such as mixers and blenders have fields induced by their motors, but since these are used for such short periods they should not be too harmful. Microwave ovens use powerful magnetrons, which produce strong magnetic fields. They cook food by agitating the molecules with very high frequencies. The reason why the cook is not cooked with the food is because, theoretically, the casing of the oven is designed to contain the microwaves. But appliances seldom perform 100 per cent efficiently and they deteriorate with use. The fact that the appliance is acknowledged to be dangerous and we have to rely on a shielding mechanism is made even more worrying when we discover that scientists in different countries advise different levels of safety. A microwave considered safe in the UK or Germany is considered unsafe in Russia. Russian scientists – respected pioneers in health – believe that anyone using a non-Russian microwave oven may become ill. They specify radiation levels that are up to one thousand times lower than those specified in the USA. Such divergent views about safety standards should give cause for concern. Have your microwave checked regularly for electromagnetic leakage.

PRECAUTIONARY MEASURES

There are many uncertainties on the issues raised by electric and electromagnetic fields and no one can establish the extent to which they will be susceptible. But anyone who has persistent symptoms of illness not attributable to any known cause, or who may be wondering about their lack of energy, might be wise to at least give these matters consideration.

It is possible to buy or hire detectors which can identify 'hot spots' of electromagnetic activity in indoor environments. Electromagnetic fields are measured in milligauss. Since research on this issue is at an early stage, there are no clear guidelines about safe strength of fields, and the question of what is practical is also relevant. A level of 2 milligauss appears to be a reasonably achievable maximum, below which it appears there is less likelihood of risk. Use measuring devices to establish the strengths of fields. If you detect fields in the order of 2 milligauss and above in areas where anyone spends much time you might wish to consider some of the following to minimize risks:

▶ Limit the time you spend in areas containing these electromagnetic fields.

▶ Since it is difficult to manage without any electrical equipment, ensure that those you have comply with current safety standards.

▶ Have microwave ovens checked annually.

▶ Arrange furniture so that field-generating equipment is as far away as possible from positions where people spend any length of time. Don't forget equipment on the other side of a wall.

▶ For mobile phones and other appliances that you do need to be close to, keep their use as brief as possible.

▶ Make sure that children do not sit or lie within one metre of a television screen.

▶ Do not leave television or audio equipment on 'standby'.

▶ Do not seat anyone close to the back of a VDU, where the fields are strongest.

▶ Try to avoid placing beds on walls adjacent to, or on floors immediately above, incoming electricity mains, fuseboards or consumer units.

▶ Bed-heads should be at least one metre from electrical sockets and equipment such as radio alarms.

▶ If you do use an electric blanket, unplug it rather than switch it off on the lead.

▶ To shield your body from electrical stress when in bed, it is possible to obtain a protective sheet to lay under the mattress. It is claimed that this will attract all surrounding electrical fields and run them to earth.

▶ Consider installation of demand switches (see p.104) on bedroom circuits.

Chapter Three

MATERIALS

FLOORING

THE FLOOR IS POSSIBLY THE SINGLE MOST IMPORTANT factor in establishing the feel and quality of a room. From a practical point of view, it is the first surface you should choose. Flooring is subject to more stringent demands than any other surface and, since it is both difficult and costly to change, you need to make sure it will meet your practical and aesthetic requirements. Get your floor right and it will give you endless satisfaction; get it wrong and it will be a daily headache.

Floors also play a crucial role in creating healthy indoor air. Not only is the floor the largest dirt-collecting surface, but it can also be a source of dirt: the abrasive action of feet degrades the surface and adds to the amount of particulates in the air. These settle on the floor and are stirred up when walked on. A healthy floor is a clean floor – whatever it is made of. There is no doubt that a clean carpet will be healthier than a dirty hard floor, but the general view is that harder floors, provided they are kept clean, are safer. In global environmental terms, most flooring materials require considerable resources, so it is worth seeking out those made of recycled materials.

CHOOSING YOUR FLOOR

The range of floor coverings is so vast and making the right choice is so important that it is useful to work through this checklist when trying to reach a decision:

1. Look at the nature and condition of the existing floor structure to establish the possible options:
▶ Will the structure take a heavy flooring material?
▶ Are there level problems that might limit the thickness of a floor covering?
▶ Does the covering need to prevent transfer of noise through the structure to rooms below?
▶ Is the floor so uneven that a thin covering will wear at high spots?
2. Determine the demands that the floor must satisfy:
▶ Will the floor have to cope with water, grease or excessive dirt?
▶ Is it an area that will get a lot of rough use?
▶ Will people walk barefoot on the floor?
▶ Will children play on it?
3. Consider the look and feel you want in the space and what other needs the flooring might need to address:
▶ Is the acoustic quality of the flooring important?
▶ Do you want a floor that reflects light to make a brighter room?
▶ Do you want a floor that absorbs solar gain?
(See p.48 and pp.66–67 for the ways in which floors affect the temperature, light and acoustic properties of a room.)

Once you have decided on possible options that might be suitable, you should then assess these for their environmental performance, and how they meet the criteria listed in chapter one (see pp.34–7). The chart on p.122–3 summarizes the qualities of different materials from an environmental point of view. As every material is different, it is important to take account of the qualifying notes, as well as the particulars of your own installation.

The most successful floors are those that appear to be part of the structure of the building. In traditional buildings, flooring was generally made of a material found in the surroundings – brick, ceramic or stone flags in a rural area, or timber boards for homes near woodland. In an urban area, stone related to the building material looks best. However fine a material may be, it may not look right if it is out of context with its surroundings.

STONE

Stone, including marble and slate, is one of the most beautiful and environmentally sound flooring materials. It has no adverse effect on internal air quality and satisfies most environmental criteria: it is easily available, requires very little energy for its extraction, and gives off no polluting emissions in production. It is also immensely durable and can be recycled again and again. Even if discarded, it will cause no pollution. However, select a stone that is relatively local to avoid using energy in transport.

TIMBER FLOORING

A timber floor is warm and reflects
light. It also makes a perfect
background for colourful rugs.

The main environmental question to think about when considering stone flooring is whether the material is being depleted or the landscape being destroyed through the stone's extraction. Generally, stone is unlikely to be exhausted, except in rare examples of specialist types such as Portland or Purbeck stone, but it is difficult to assess the effect that quarrying may have in far-flung countries. One way of ensuring reasonable environmental credentials for stone is to source it from areas in which it can be assumed that there are legal environmental controls in place to regulate extraction.

In design terms, stone is an attractive, practical flooring material. It is often thought to be cold, but a stone floor needs only the addition of a soft rug for comfort and warmth. Stone is also ideal for use with underfloor heating systems – its density allows it to store heat well and to radiate it very efficiently.

CERAMIC, BRICKS AND TILES

For centuries, fired clay has been used all over the world to make floors, in forms ranging from simple, sun-baked bricks to elaborate glazed tiles. One of the most attractive features of traditional ceramic tiles made of local clay is that they bring regional characteristics to interiors – think of French farmhouse tiles or tiled floors in Italian palazzos.

Ceramic tiles rate very highly from an environmental point of view. Ceramic material (clay) exists in abundance and its processing is generally simple, relatively clean and uses few chemicals. In large-scale commercial production, gas-fired kilns are often used, but in 'native' production, wood is more common. Small quantities of heavy metals are used for colouring glazes, but the total level of pollution is relatively low compared to that associated with many building materials. In terms of indoor air quality, ceramic material is stable and quite safe.

CLASSIC FLOORS

A combination of glazed and unglazed tiles combine into a simple pattern with a decorative border (left). Stone slabs have such character that they are perfect on their own and need no other adornment (above).

Clay tiles are made waterproof by being fired at high temperatures – the higher the temperature, the denser and more waterproof the result. This firing process is called vitrification. Fully vitrified tiles are hard and completely waterproof. They are also known as quarry tiles.

Traditional red terracotta is fired to a relatively low temperature, which makes soft tiles. Although common in Mediterranean homes and other traditional buildings, unvitrified tiles are less practical because they are not waterproof and are subject to frost damage. Low fired tiles can be waterproofed by glazing with either transparent or coloured glazes. Common examples are glazed bathroom tiles or the decorative tiles of Moorish Spain.

Tiles are almost indestructible and can be used time and time again – in fact, they may well command higher prices when worn, further ensuring their reuse. At the end of their life they can either be formed into mosaics of broken tiles, (see p.168), used as hardcore layers on building sites, or crushed to make safe sands.

MOSAIC, TERRAZZO AND CONCRETE

Mosaic was traditionally made from small pieces of marble or glass (still known by the Latin term *tesserae*) set into a bedding on a solid floor. This art form reached its zenith in Ravenna between 400 and 600 AD, when glass artists used coloured pieces of unsurpassed brilliance, including gold and silver. The technique of setting small objects into a bedding today still lends itself to endless inventiveness and is an ideal way of recycling materials. Almost any object flat enough to make a floor can be used – coins, sea shells, bones and mechanical components. The health and environmental credentials of the finished floor depend on the material used (see the information in this chapter) and also on the materials used for the bedding.

BRICK (left), SLATE (above), TERRACOTTA (below)

POLISHED CONCRETE

Plain materials have an attractive simplicity. Here, polished concrete flooring is an ideal partner for the rich hardwood on the stairs (left).

OLD AND NEW MOSAICS

The traditional mosaic (below) is made of tiny *tesserae* tiles. The simple plain stone tiles (bottom) are combined with mosaic pebble stripes to make an unusual floor.

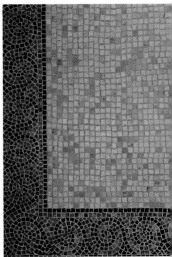

Mosaic floors have many practical and environmental advantages: they are hard-wearing, can act as a heat sink for solar gain, and offer good opportunities for using discarded and recycled materials. With all the opportunities it offers for imaginative and attractive designs, mosaic flooring deserves much more widespread use in the home than it currently enjoys.

A polished bare cement or concrete floor is simple and attractive. Its colour can be enhanced by adding marble chips or dust to the wet floor, which is then ground to a smooth finish. This is known as terrazzo flooring. It can be coved up the walls to form an integral skirting, and creates a hard-wearing, stain-resistant and waterproof surface – ideal in bathrooms and areas of heavy wear. Concrete and terrazzo score highly from an environmental point of view: although concrete is a high-energy product, these floors maximize the use of the main structure and avoid the need for additional finishes and coatings. However, they can only be used where the structural floor itself is concrete. Mosaic, concrete and terrazzo are all ideal for use with underfloor heating.

SOLID WOODEN FLOORING

Solid wood is beautiful, practical and has for centuries made some of the finest floors. It meets all the main requirements for an environmentally sound surface – it is a renewable resource, requires low-energy input, and is safe and biodegradable. It is also one of the easiest materials to recycle. Timbers can be grouped under three headings:
▶ Softwoods
▶ Sustainable hardwoods
▶ Protected tropical and temperate hardwoods
Softwoods come from coniferous trees such as pine, larch, European redwood (not the Californian sequoias) and spruce. These grow mainly in the northern hemisphere, from Canada right across northern Europe and Russia. Relatively fast growing – a softwood crop can be taken in approximately 20 years – they are used for most wooden construction, floors and furniture as well for the engineered boards described below.

Sustainable hardwoods grow mainly in North America, Europe and Asia. They come from broadleaf forests that are managed to ensure a continuity of regeneration and supply of such timbers as oak, ash, maple and sycamore. It is not commonly known that some old-growth temperate forests in North America and Asia are now being destroyed.

Tropical hardwoods come from tropical rainforests in South and Central America, Africa and Asia. A few are managed for proper regeneration, but others come from unregulated harvesting and should never be used. Teak, iroko, mahoganies and aformosia are among the better known of the protected species. These trees are essential to the stability of the rainforest habitat and their removal causes ecological collapse, resulting in the loss of unique flora and fauna and consequent soil erosion, leading to the transformation of a once immensely rich forest system into desert. This in turn destroys indigenous communities, as well the world's last great resource of natural plant chemicals – a gene bank that may disappear before the potential of these substances is discovered.

There are accreditation schemes for tropical hardwoods, but many of these are dubious and simply used as marketing aids. The only schemes that are reliable are those recognized by the Forestry Stewardship Council (FSC), which operates internationally (see p.195).

Essential points to consider when laying a timber floor include:
▶ Select only certified hardwoods or softwoods and preferably timber that is locally produced.
▶ Don't use timber in areas where it would require heavy protection against wear and water.
▶ Use only natural oils and waxes as finishes (see p 138).
▶ Use recycled flooring wherever possible.

COMPOSITE AND ENGINEERED FLOORING

A wide range of products known as 'engineered timber' is made up in various ways to look like solid timber. These products include:
▶ Boards with a face of solid timber (2–6 mm thick) glued to particle board backing
▶ Boards with a very thin (maximum 1 mm) veneer of timber glued to a particle board backing
▶ Particle boards printed with a photo of wood grain
▶ Sheets that contain no timber but are made of plastic and printed with a photo to emulate timber
Some of the above products come unfinished and can be

RECYCLED FLOORBOARDS
The interesting patina of age and wear adds to the effect of colour, grain and texture to make reused floorboards an attractive feature in any room (left).

HERRINGBONE PATTERN
Short boards as well as full-length timbers can be reused. This herringbone pattern makes best use of short lengths but requires careful craftsmanship (right).

finished on site. Others have a factory-applied finish, such as a thick clear vinyl film, over the timber veneer. Only those floors with proper timber veneer create the look, sound and feel of real timber. Some of the better products are indistinguishable from timber, even on close scrutiny.

These boards can be as thin as 9 mm, for laying over existing floors, and are generally, but not always, cheaper than solid wood. Overlay flooring is also available with a rubber backing that is made from recycled tyres. The advantage of using a resilient layer is that it will accommodate unevenness in the subfloor and provides some acoustic insulation (see p.88).

The environmental aspects of these timbers are not straightforward and depend on all their different elements – veneer, backing material, resins and finish.

▶ Veneer is not significantly different from solid timber, except that much less timber is used.

▶ Particle- and chipboards should be assessed in terms of the type of wood particles used (usually wood waste), and the glues and bonding resins.

▶ Finishing coats of clear vinyl have the same poor environmental characteristics as sheet vinyl (see p.122)

▶ For the environmental aspects of liquid-applied finishes see p.138.

BAMBOO

Although it is a grass, bamboo is as strong as many timbers and almost as dense and hard-wearing indoors as oak. Like all grass, bamboo grows quickly – as much as 2.4 metres every year. This means that pieces of a usable size are

STAINED WOOD
Timber flooring can be stained in a light colour to create a durable, easy to care for floor that also reflects light (right).

generated from crops every five or six years – roughly six times faster than wood. Other great advantages of bamboo are that it grows on marginal land, does not need fertilizers or pesticides and is a coppice crop – it regrows from cut shoots and does not have to be replanted.

For centuries, bamboo has been used in its natural form as strong, flexible sticks. Now that its excellent environmental characteristics have been recognized, bamboo is being used more and more as a versatile and attractive flooring material. Just as timber is engineered into a number of forms, bamboo can be engineered into narrow or wide boards or panels, exposing either the face, the end or the long-edge grain. Thick boards can be tongue-and-grooved for use in the same way as timber in making a structural floor on joists or on battens laid over concrete. Thinner boards can also be used as overlay flooring, in the same way as timber (see p.115). From the point of view of internal air quality, bamboo has the same advantages as other smooth surfaces, provided that no unsafe coatings or adhesives are applied.

CORK

Cork comes from the bark of the cork oak and has been cultivated in Mediterranean countries for centuries. An entirely sustainable crop, it is harvested from live trees that regrow their bark to give a new crop approximately every nine years. Cork is an excellent flooring material. Its combination of flexibility, high insulation value and resistance to water is a product of its structure in which fatty materials make each cell a watertight compartment. It is ideal for areas where a combination of warmth and some water resistance is needed, such as bathrooms or playrooms.

Cork is available in tiles made from small granules, larger flakes or slices bonded together with adhesive resins. Tiles usually measure 30 x 30 cm by 3 mm thick but planks of 90 x 18 cm x 6 mm are also available. The quality of cork tiles varies and their durability depends largely on the quality of the bonding adhesives used. It is difficult to verify this on purchase, however, and the safest course of action is to use a reputable manufacturer. Beware of knock-down bargain offers.

Cork is a little warmer and softer than lino, but less durable. As with so many other natural flooring materials,

BAMBOO

Fast-growing bamboo has long been used to make furniture. Strips are now also assembled into planks for use as an environmentally friendly flooring material (above).

SAFE FLOORING

Bamboo (below) and palm wood (below left) both make hard-wearing, attractive floors. They are easy to keep clean and give off no harmful chemicals.

cork's practicality and its effects on indoor air quality and health are affected largely by the finish. It degrades easily if not protected with a durable hard-wearing coat, and discolours if the protection is penetrated by water. Cork flooring is available unfinished, with a variety of factory-applied acrylic or polyurethane coatings or a clear vinyl surface sheet.Ideally, use tiles that are partly finished with a solvent-free coating and then apply further coats of the same material after installation. All edges and joints should be sealed. Cork can be glued to either timber or concrete structural floors, but always make sure that you use a safe adhesive (see p.196).

CARPET

Fitted or edge-to-edge carpet, though not fashionable in recent years, has many advantages. It can turn an 'unfriendly' room into a warm and welcoming space. Soft and comfortable underfoot, it provides warmth as well as acoustic softness. No hard floor is as comfortable for children to play on, or for walking on barefoot in winter, and a thick carpet and underlay will also deaden impact noise (see p.90). In older houses with draughty ground floors, carpet stops draughts and increases warmth. It can also cover floors of a poor or uneven quality.

Carpet is also one of the easiest floorings to maintain, provided one has a good vacuum cleaner. Because of its natural oiliness, wool has some natural resistance to stains, which makes woollen carpet ideal even in areas of heavy use. (Avoid stain resistance treatments (see p.149).

Good quality carpet can last for many years. The best combination for longevity is generally considered to be 80 per cent wool to 20 per cent nylon. Artificial fibres may be extremely hard-wearing, but are unsafe in production and also tend to 'ugly out' before natural fibres, loosing their colour or pattern. This is generally because artificial fibres take colour less well than natural ones, which is why they are so difficult to dye.

Against all these benefits must be weighed a number of concerns about carpet:
▶ Carpet is generally considered to be one of the worst culprits in creating poor indoor air quality, harbouring invisible particulates as well as dust mite faeces, which thrive in the warmth of carpet.

CORK
Cork is a safe, versatile flooring material (above). It is warm to walk on and also helps to soften the acoustics in a room.

RUSH FLOORING
Traditional rush flooring is warm and has a wonderful textured look (below). It is ideal on old stone floors because it can tolerate damp.

Natural grass flooring gives a soft,
but heavily textured finish on this
staircase and landing (left).

▶ First industrial age production, even of natural woollen
carpet, is highly damaging because of the extensive use of
dangerous and polluting chemicals during all stages of
production. The yarns in synthetic carpet are made from
petrochemicals, with all the disadvantages outlined in
chapter one (see pp. 30–1).

▶ Chemically treated natural and synthetic carpets are a
major constituent of waste in landfill sites. They do not
biodegrade and leach out polluting chemicals.

CARPET BACKINGS AND UNDERLAYS

Many carpets have backings that are treated with anti-
aging chemicals and adhesives made of styrene butadiene
rubber (SBR), which is carcinogenic and should be avoided.
In some high-quality carpets, the backing is woven into
the pile not glued, which is preferable but expensive.
Underlays should ideally be made from untreated woollen
felt matting or recycled rubber.

Some manufacturers recommend that their carpets be
glued to the floor, but this is a very unsound practice. A
large amount of adhesive is used and when the carpet
eventually has to be ripped up and thrown away, the floor
surface cannot be used again for a different finish without
considerable work. Low-tack glues that are meant to avoid
this problem are now available, but they are only partly
successful, and they too are generally solvent-based. A
better solution is to use edge-gripper rods.

ENVIRONMENTALLY SAFE CARPET

It is possible to obtain carpet with relatively low impact on
the environment. So called 'organic' carpet, made from
natural plant and animal yarns, is pesticide free and not
bleached or chemically dyed. The natural oil of lanolin in
wool is retained as a water and stain repellent. Wool is also
self-extinguishing and needs no fire-retardant chemical
applications. The yarns are woven onto backings made of
chemical-free jute or hemp. Hemp is increasingly being

used in environmentally sound carpets because it has a natural resistance to mildew and fungal growth, and to fading. Generally non-toxic adhesives are used – often natural latex rubber.

Carpets from vegetable yarns such as jute, coir and sisal are also available in a range of natural colours, free from any dyes. Although they are often sold as 'natural' they won't be chemical free unless this is stated to be the case. Natural fibre carpets that are not chemically treated score particularly well with regard to renewability of resource, embodied energy and their ability to biodegrade (see p.122–3).

A new environmentally safe floor covering is made from paper twine, woven with linen into carpet widths and mats. Thinner than carpet, it has a texture not dissimilar to a very fine cane weave, and is available in an attractive range of natural, earthy tones woven into checked and striped patterns. A non-slip surface made of water-based synthetic latex is applied to the back of the flooring. Closed-loop production methods (see p.31) have greatly increased opportunities for making environmentally sound synthetic carpet. Carpet made from recycled plastic

UNDYED CARPET

This undyed carpet has an ribbed surface that catches the light. It needs no colour or pattern (above).

PAPER TWINE

Paper twine matting makes a soft but durable flooring that can be used on old damp surfaces (below).

drink bottles made of PET (polyethelyene terapthalate) that would otherwise occupy landfill sites is also coming into production.

CARPET AND INDOOR AIR QUALITY

The chemicals involved in carpet and underlay production can contribute to poor air quality. As with textiles, the manufacturing process involves a wide range of chemicals that remain as residues in the fibres (see p.144). Backings and adhesives, with potential offgassing, present further health hazards. The smell of new carpet is in fact the off-gassing of VOCs, which can continue for up to six months. Many cases of fatigue, eye or mucous membrane irritation in office environments have been attributed to new carpet.

When buying carpets, choose products certified by the the CIR (Carpet and Rug Institute Indoor Air Quality Testing) label in the USA, or the GUT standard in Europe as being safe. However, compliance with the limits set by these agencies does not necessarily mean products are totally problem free.

PRECAUTIONS WHEN INSTALLING NEW CARPET

▶ Ask the supplier/installer to unroll and air the carpet before delivery to your home.
▶ Open all windows and doors during and after installation, and if possible run a fan to dissipate fumes.
▶ Do not occupy the room for up to 72 hours after laying – or while there is still the residual odour from the carpet and adhesives.
▶ Vacuum the carpet thoroughly before using the room.
▶ Don't leave a baby to sleep in a room with a carpet that is less than six months old.

RUGS

The best way to enjoy a safe floor and the softness and warmth of carpet without laying fitted carpet is to use rugs. Easy to remove for thorough cleaning (areas under furniture collect the most dust), they can also be rolled

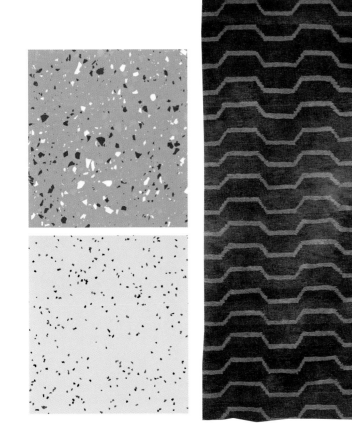

RECYCLED RUBBER

Rubber flooring, made mainly from recycled materials (far left), comes in a variety of colours and patterns.

ETHICAL PRODUCTION

This modern, boldly patterned rug was woven in Tibet using local wools and dyes (left). The makers certify that their rugs are produced by workers with acceptable labour conditions.

away at times when lots of dirt is being brought into the home by pets or muddy children. Flat-weave rugs such as kelims have no pile, so they harbour less dust than those with thick pile. Rugs last longer if placed on an underlay. And since the underlay is separate, it is also easy to clean. A point to note is that rug weaving in many parts of the world involves child labour and poor working conditions. Whenever possible, buy ethically certified rugs.

RUBBER

Rubber sheet or tile flooring is durable, scuff resistant and easy to maintain. It comes in a range of colours and textures, including round studs and a variety of raised grid patterns, which make it particularly useful in areas where a non-slip surface is needed. It is also more resilient than other sheet materials and has better acoustic qualities.

Good-quality rubber flooring can contain 75 per cent of natural rubber derived from trees and 25 per cent of synthetic (petrochemical) rubbers, fillers and pigments. The Danish Environmental Protection Agency recommends a material known as EPDM as the safest synthetic rubber. While the process of production does require high levels of energy, it is relatively low in emissions and waste. In the best quality rubber flooring, pigments are usually vegetable or mineral based. Offgassing is very low and the flooring can be recycled into lower-grade rubber products such as safety mats.

Rubber flooring can also be made from recycled car tyres. These are ground, added to coloured rubber granules and reformed under heat and pressure into the basis for sheet or tiles. Few pollutants are given off and the environmental benefits of using discarded tyres are clear.

LINOLEUM

Once confined to dull colours, this warm, flexible and eminently practical material is now available in brighter shades, thanks to improvements in binder and pigment technology. Linoleum is made from entirely natural ingredients: linum is the flax from which the base is woven, and 'oleum' refers to the oils used – usually linseed and pine resins. Fillers of cork and ground-up wood waste are also safe and renewable. Production produces few polluting emissions and linoleum is also biodegradable. High temperatures are required during the 'calendering' process, which makes the surface dense and smooth, but lino has far fewer environmental consequences than many sheet materials. It is claimed to be naturally bactericidal.

In use, lino is is an ideal material for the safe home – it is hard-wearing, stain resistant and easy to keep clean. It is suitable for areas that may be splashed with water, although it becomes slippery when wet. It can be used wherever a flat, impervious sheet is needed and it is slightly softer and more resilient than PVC sheet flooring or tiles. Linoleum offers many attractive characteristics for use in all areas. Where a touch of softness is needed, linoleum is an excellent background for loose rugs.

VINYL (POLYVINYLCHLORIDE) FLOORING

In use, PVC flooring is similar to linoleum, except that it is less resilient. However, PVC is most unsatisfactory from an environmental point of view because it is derived from crude oil and requires large amounts of energy and chlorine to manufacture, although some chlorine-free PVCs are becoming available. PVC also contains dangerous chemicals such as pthalates. It is claimed that these are 'trapped in the chemical makeup and do not leach or escape during the use of the floor'. While this may be true, the very use of such chemicals makes this synthetic flooring questionable when other excellent products available.

In addition, PVC is virtually indestructible unless it is incinerated, when it gives off dangerous toxic emissions. If left in landfill, it leaches chlorine and heavy metal into the ground. PVC is so problematic that a number of German municipalities have banned its use.

NEW RECYCLED FLOORING MATERIALS

In addition to recycled rubber, other flooring materials made from recycled products are coming onto the market. Recycled glass is used with ceramic materials to make dense, stain-resistant tiles. They are similar to glazed tiles but are fired at relatively low temperatures, and the process involves no toxic emissions. A United Nations programme to discover sustainable products has also developed a floor tile made from ground mussel shells set in a cement compound, but these are not yet on the market.

FLOORING CHART

This summarizes in broad terms the environmental and practical aspects of different flooring materials.

✔ Good rating
○ Medium rating
✘ Poor rating

FUNCTIONAL CRITERIA

	DURABILITY	STAIN RESISTANCE	DURABILITY IN WET AREAS
CARPET (WOOL)[3]	○	○	✘
CARPET (ORGANIC)	○	○	✘
CARPET (SYNTHETIC)[3]	○	○	○
GRASSES/RUSHES[3]	✘	✘	✘
LINOLEUM[3]	✔	✔	✔
VINYL[3]	✔	✔	✔
CORK[3]	○	○	○
RUBBER[3]	✔	✔	✔
SOFTWOOD	○	○	○
EUROPEAN & US HARDWOOD[8]	✔	✔	✔[4]
TROPICAL HARDWOOD[8]	✔	✔	✔
CERAMIC[3]	✔	✔	✔
MOSAIC[3]	✔	✔	✔
STONE	✔	✔	✔

1. Some synthetic carpet is recycled.
2. Depends also on distance transported from source to user.
3. Depends also on adhesives used.
4. Oak is very durable but discolours when wet.

5. Can be dangerous on stairs if it becomes worn.
6. No material is slip resistant if covered with a film of water.
7. Available with rough surfaces to reduce slip.
8. Only sustainable timbers considered.

ENVIRONMENTAL CRITERIA

SOFTNESS	WARMTH	SLIP RESISTANCE[6]	SOUND ABSORBENCY	RESOURCE DEPLETION	EMBODIED ENERGY[2]	EMISSIONS DURING MANUFACTURE	EFFECT ON INDOOR AIR[3]	CAPACITY FOR RECYCLING/ BIODEGRADING
✓	✓	✓[5]	✓	✓	✓	○	✗	○
✓	✓	✓[5]	✓	✓	✓	✓	✗	✓
○	○	✓[5]	✓	✗[1]	✗	✗[1]	✗	✗[1]
○	○	✓[5]	✓	✓	✓	✓	✗	✓
○	○	✗	○	✓	○	✓	✓	✓
✗	✗	✗[7]	✗	✗	✗	✗	✗	✗
○	○	○	✓	✓	✓	✓	✓	✓
○	○	○[7]	○	○	○	○	○	○
○	✓	○	○	✓	✓	✓	✓	✓
✗	✓	○	○	○	✓	✓	✓	✓
✗	○	○	○	✓	✓	✓	✓	✓
✗	✗	✗[7]	✗	✓	✓	✓	✓	✓
✗	✗	✗	✗	✓	✓	✓	✓	✓
✗	✗	✗	✗	○	✓	✓	✓	✓

WALL LININGS

WALLS ARE THE LARGEST SURFACE AREA IN ANY SPACE. Wall linings, such as panelling, tiles, wallpaper or tapestries, allow us to modify the walls that we have to ensure that they are as environmentally sound and attractive as possible. The surfaces and texture of walls affect a space in the following ways:

▶ Their ability to radiate cool or heat into or out of the room.

▶ Their ability to absorb or reflect light.

▶ Whether they create a hard or soft acoustic quality.

▶ Their smell and effect on indoor air quality.

▶ Their ability to 'breathe'.

Traditionally, the rough walls of dwellings could be covered with linings to make them draughtproof, warm, smooth and easier to keep clean. But it is worth considering whether additional coverings on walls today are necessary. Working on the environmental principle that less is best, omitting wall linings may be safest both for the planet and your personal health. This consideration, of course, needs to be weighed against the extent to which the addition of wall linings might enhance the environmental performance of a dwelling. The nature of the basic structure is crucial in this – if the walls are smooth and warm, any other addition should be minimal. If, on the other hand, you can increase insulation, reduce draughts, or improve the comfort of your home, then applied wall linings have a great deal to offer.

RIGID PANELLING

Timber has long been one of the most widely used of wall linings. Available locally, it is relatively lightweight, easy to apply, and offers an attractive surface for decorating. The insulating qualities of timber make panelled walls warm and pleasant to the touch. Traditional panels were made from whatever timber was to hand. The great houses of Europe employed the finest craftsmen to carve elaborate designs such as linenfold panelling in oak from their own estates, while modest cottages had panels of thin, rough boards taken from nearby woodland. Both helped to create warm rooms, in which the timber was decoration in itself.

Wall panelling or boarding is best fixed to timber battens on the wall, packed out where necessary to create a flat plane. Such linings add to the insulation of a room. You can improve the insulation further by lining the back of any panelling with insulating material, but to avoid condensation problems, don't pack the space so tightly that there is no room for air movement. Use environmentally safe insulation material, including paper, shredded flax, sheep's wool, cork and coconut fibre. A reflective surface of aluminium foil facing into an air gap behind panelling can also improve thermal performance and avoids the danger of trapping condensation if ventilation is inadequate. Aluminium foil is generally made from recycled aluminium and is therefore relatively benign.

Wall panelling offers the opportunity to solve visual problems such as uneven surfaces or half-buried pipes. It can also be integrated with cupboard fronts or even doorways to create complete panelled walls. If you treat the panelling as independent from the line of the existing walls, you can reshape rooms with curves and angled planes so as to create spaces in which to hide storage units and equipment such as televisions and stereos. This is a particularly useful approach in rooms that have several functions such as home-offices.

The void between the existing structural wall and the new inner lining, whether narrow or wide, forms a useful temperature buffer zone that ameliorates extremes of outside heat or cold. Avoiding condensation is essential, so you must maintain an air flow through any such space by leaving gaps at the bottom and top of linings and ensuring that any battens or internal shelves do not block the air

WOODEN WALLS
Wooden boards line the walls of this room, providing warmth and an attractive textured surface.

flow. Larger voids should have air bricks or vents to bring air from the outside.

Although wall panelling can be made economically from engineered boards, many of these are not environmentally sound (see p.113). Given that the boards will probably be used over a large area, particular care should be taken to check that they will not damage indoor air quality. Softer fibreboards (check these for urea and formaldehyde glues) can be useful for softening the acoustics in a room, and add some degree of heat insulation to colder walls. They are not very durable as a wall surface, however, and are most suitable for use as pinboard, possibly covered with fabric.

The choice of timber, whether painted or veneered board (see p.113), affects the atmosphere of a room. Darker oak timbers or the rich reds of cherry provide a warm, luxurious feel, while light oak, ash, maple and pines give a brighter look. Wood can add an attractive scent – either from its natural resins or from natural wax polishes or oils (see p.138). Panelling can also be made from bamboo – a durable material which meets many environmental criteria (see pp. 115–16).

CORK AND LINOLEUM

Cork designed for use on walls tends to be softer than floor cork and has a more open texture. It is available in a wide range of colours and provides excellent thermal insulation, as well as softening the sound quality in a space. Cork is ideal in basements to counter the cold and often echoey feel associated with the hard finishes that may have been used on walls. It is also good for children's rooms, where it softens the sound and provides a perfect surface for putting up pictures and posters. Light, natural corks can be stained with coloured wood stains.

Linoleum is also available in a softer grade for walls and makes an attractive surface. Use linoleum on bathroom walls for a water-resistant surface without the hardness of ceramic tiles. The flexibility of linoleum allows it to be taken around corners to avoid joints.

CERAMIC TILES

Ceramic finishes on walls provide hard, impervious surfaces with a harsh acoustic. They generally give a cold feel

LINENFOLD PANELLING
Oak panelling, intricately carved with a traditional linenfold pattern, lines the cold stone walls of many old homes (below). Other materials used in the room are also natural.

TILED WALLS
Glazed terracotta tiles make an attractive wallcovering that is hardwearing, washable and generally safe (right). Their cool surface is ideal in warmer climates.

– welcome in hot climates, where tiled walls create cool and restful interiors. Ceramic tiles for use on walls tend to be thinner than floor tiles and can be larger as they are not subject to as much impact or weight. The advantages of tiles are that they are durable, waterproof and available in a wide range of colours and patterns. (For information on the environmental aspects of ceramic material see p.110.) The effect of ceramic tiles on indoor air quality depends largely on the adhesives used.

PLASTERS

Wall plasters made of clay, lime and gypsum have since the earliest times been used to block draughty cracks and

SIMPLE PLASTER

Raw plaster can be an attractive finish without the need for any paintwork and requires very little maintenance (above).

A QUIET SPACE

This stunning, restful space is given its individual richness and texture by the grass linings used on the walls and ceiling (right).

create smooth surfaces. Clay, in particular, is not only the oldest, but also perhaps the most environmentally sound of any material – it accounts for about 70 per cent of earth. It can be dug virtually anywhere, requires no energy to process, is stable, benign and biodegrades.

Forgotten for generations, clay plasters are now coming into use again. Designed to be left undecorated, they are available in a range of subtle earth colours, with textures varying from smooth to rough. Some clay plasters can even be applied in layers as thin as 3 mm on masonry. If applying clay to plasterboard, an adhesive priming coat is needed to ensure that it sticks. Provided that clay plaster is applied to a thick (25 mm) backing coat, it helps to create good indoor air quality – it is vapour permeable and absorbs excessive humidity, so helping to prevent damp. Clay plasters are particularly appropriate for use when renovating old, damp masonry buildings.

An interesting new development in France is a plaster made from hemp and mixed with natural lime and water. It can be applied by trowel or poured into moulds to make flowing forms, like a lightweight concrete. Furthermore, the hemp gives it a slight resilience somewhat like that of

cork, with all the advantages of warmth and acoustic soft-ness. One of the most important environmental benefits of using clay or hemp plasters is that because they have an attractive natural colour you can reduce the consumption of resources by eliminating painting entirely. If you do want to colour wash clay plasters, they combine well with lime paints (see p.136) to make a 'breathing' wall.

PAPER, FABRIC AND VINYL WALL LININGS
Paper wall coverings date from fifteenth-century Europe, when single sheets of paper were glued to the walls to form decorative patterns and designs. Walls were also papered for health reasons – coverings were called 'sanitary papers' because their oil-based inks made it possible for walls to be washed. Wallpapers were used extensively until about the middle of the twentieth century, with craftsmen printers and artists of international standing such as William Morris and Owen Jones providing designs for mass-produced papers. Today, the use of wallpapers and similar coverings is questionable, since they use resources and processing but have no environmental benefit. With the wide range of safe and durable plasters and paints

available to meet most demands, it is sounder to eliminate the paper and apply any decorative colour or pattern directly to the wall.

Papers are made of three principal elements, each of which may have environmental consequences: the face material, which can range from printed papers to grasses and silks; the backing materials, usually paper; and the adhesives. Dyes and inks used in the face material are often dangerous, as are the mould inhibitors included to prevent microbial growth in the paper in the event of dampness.

Wallpaper manufacturers have developed a standard for papers that establishes their environmental safety and this is stamped onto papers. The standard ensures the avoidance of the following substances: monomer vinyl chlorides, formaldehyde, lead, cadmium, CFCs and volatile plasticizers. Safer papers are becoming available that are made with as much as 60 per cent of recycled materials. The Forestry Stewardship Council (see p.195) also certifies some papers which use renewable timber sources. Fabric wall coverings should be subject to the many questions applied to fabric production (see p.144).

More common now than wallpaper are vinyl wall coverings, popular because of their durability and economy. Vinyl is derived from petrochemicals, and its processing includes dangerous plasticizers, chlorines and synthetic inks and dyes. Vinyl wall coverings are impermeable so, in

---

✔ Good rating
◯ Medium rating
✗ Poor rating

1. Depends also on distance transported from source to user.
2. May be affected by amount of recycled material included.
3. Will be affected by material used for backing.

4. Will depend on chemicals used.
5. Will also depend on adhesives used.
6. Only sustainable timbers considered

	FUNCTIONAL CRITERIA				ENVIRONMENTAL CRITERIA	
	THERMAL INSULATION	SOUND ABSORBENCY[3]	DURABILITY WHEN WET	DURABILITY WHEN ABRADED	RESOURCE DEPLETION[2]	EMBODIED ENERGY [1]
PAPER [3]	✗	✗	✗	✗	✗	✗
FABRIC & GRASS WALLPAPERS[3]	✗	✗	✗	✗	◯	✗
THICK WEAVES/ TAPESTRIES FELT	◯	✔	✗	✗	◯	✔
VINYL	✗	✗	◯	✔	✗	✗
THICK GRASS/ BAMBOOS	◯	✔	◯	◯	✔	✔
SOFTWOOD	✔	◯	◯	◯	✔	✔
EUROPEAN & US HARDWOOD[6]	✔	◯	✔	✔	◯	✔
TROPICAL HARDWOOD[6]	✔	◯	✔	✔	◯	✔
CERAMIC	✗	✗	✔	✔	✔	✔
SHEET METAL	✗	✗	✔	✔	◯	✗

addition to a risk of offgassing, they also add to poor indoor air quality by contributing to condensation build-up. Although a number of companies are moving away from petrochemical plastic coverings and using less damaging materials such as wood and polyester fibres, it is best to avoid these products.

Wall covering made of woven glass shares many of the practicalities of vinyl, but is made from natural, abundant, safe materials – quartz, sand, and stone compounds. This material has the advantage of being vapour permeable, while being thick enough to cover poor wall surfaces. Woven to give a variety of attractive textures rather like those of fabric, it is designed to be overpainted.

WALL LININGS

This summarizes in broad terms the environmental and practical aspects of different wall lining materials.

...MISSIONS DURING ...ANUFACTURE	EFFECT ON INDOOR AIR [5]	CAPACITY FOR RECYCLING BIODEGRADING [5]
	◯	◯[4]
...[4]	◯	◯[4]
...[4]	✗	◯[4]
	✗	✗
	◯	✔
	✔	✔
	✔	✔
	✔	✔
	✔	✔
	✔	◯

HANGINGS AND TAPESTRIES

Fabric wall coverings were one of the most important decorative items in homes in the past, and they played a significant part in keeping cold interiors warm. In the past, fabric hangings brought colour, pattern and richness to bare rooms. Abstract patterns of flat kelim weaves hung in Bedouin tents and enormous allegorical tapestries, like the famous Bayeux Tapestry, adorned medieval castles. On stone walls, over doorways or windows, tapestries not only prevented cold radiation and offered warmth, but also made spaces glow with colour. Today, they offer all the same advantages, and the growth of craft weaving of the highest quality creates wall hangings quite as satisfying as any artwork.

While the same question arises about the environmental soundness of using yet another layer to decorate wall surfaces, hangings offer the opportunity to enhance thermal as well as acoustic properties (see p.64). The environmental aspects of fabrics are discussed on pp.144–51.

WALL HANGINGS

Tapestries and rugs hung on walls look attractive as well as adding insulation and helping to absorb sound (below).

PAINTS AND VARNISHES

BRUSH-ON COATINGS, SUCH AS PAINTS, VARNISHES and stains, cover almost every surface in our homes. Their visual effects are obvious, but they also have an invisible but dramatic impact on indoor air quality. On a global level, the manufacture and disposal of paints is a major cause of environmental pollution. This section concentrates on these aspects of brush-on coatings and suggests how their adverse effects can be minimized.

TRADITIONAL COLOURINGS

The white, lime-washed houses of Greece, the ochre-coloured walls of homes in southern France, and the brown earth tones of African houses sit so comfortably in their respective environments because their colourings come from the surrounding landscape. The materials used to make such traditional colourings included mainly ground minerals, soils, and less colour-fast pigments from crushed plants. They were made in small quantities and this, together with the particles of pigments, resulted in colours with variations of intensity and tone that are much more attractive than the uniform look of modern paints.

The use of found materials meant that paints had to be laboriously made up each time they were used, and their application was a labour-intensive and sometimes skilled task. Modern paints have been formulated to avoid these disadvantages – they require no lengthy preparation, they are quick drying, consistent in colour, economic and long lasting. But they lack richness, depth and individuality and the advantages they do have come at significant cost to our environment and personal health.

The structure of all paints is essentially the same. They have three main ingredients:
▶ Pigments that provide colour.
▶ Binding agents to make the paint adhere to the surface.
▶ Solvents, which are the carrying medium for these ingredients and allow smooth application.
They also contain a variety of additives such as fillers, opacifiers, fungicides, mould inhibitors and softeners.

MODERN SYNTHETIC PAINT PRODUCTION

The ingredients of modern synthetic paints – regardless of whether they are solvent- or water-based – derive mainly from oil-based chemicals and were developed after the discovery of aniline petrochemical derivative pigments in 1856. Thousands of chemicals are available for use in paint manufacture. Their processing uses huge amounts of fossil fuel energy and generates large quantities of waste, most of which consists of toxic emissions to air and water.

Organic solvents from paint manufacture account for approximately 20 per cent of the hydrocarbons that pollute the earth's atmosphere, and the production of 1 tonne of solvent-based paint can, in the worst cases, produce as much as 30 tonnes of dangerous, mainly toxic, non-biodegradable waste. In addition, when paint or painted surfaces are disposed of, they leach chemicals and pollute air, earth and water.

The chemicals in paint also affect air quality in the home by offgassing slowly during natural ageing, long after the initial curing period. While paint is generally considered adequately cured for practicable hardness in some 48 to 72 hours, the UK Building Research Establishment has found that all paints offgas for as long as six months, and water-based paints can do so for up to 12 months. The World Health Organization (WHO) reports that painters suffer 20 per cent more cancers than average and 40 per cent more lung cancers. PFO (perfluorocatanyl sulphate) chemicals, which have long been used in paints, have recently been recognized as serious carcinogens.

Synthetic pigments used in paint contain a wide range of substances, including unsafe quantities of heavy metals such as cadmium, titanium and cobalt, which can offgas. Solvents and binders contain substances such as synthetic

In this modern home, limewash containing a strong yellow ochre pigment adds visual interest to plain walls (right).

ORGANIC PAINTS

Organic paints (above) are safe to use and safe to live with. They also provide fresh, lively natural colours.

Synthetic paints are some of the most harmful decorating materials

turpentine and volatile organic compounds (VOCs), known to be one the most unhealthy groups of chemicals, and give rise to a variety of health problems. In general terms, the more durable the paint, the higher the solvent content. The oil-based paints normally used on woodwork and in kitchens and other areas of heavy wear have the highest solvent content. Each can of conventional synthetic oil paint can consist of as much as 70 per cent of these solvents. Matt emulsion water-based paints for walls may contain as little as 2 per cent of solvents, but they do contain other dangerous chemicals such as toxic monomers.

The paint industry in both the USA and Europe is beginning to phase out high-VOC paints. In Europe, some paints are now classified according to their VOC content, which is identified on the label in the following way:

▶ Minimal: 0-2.9 per cent
▶ Low: 3–7.99 per cent
▶ Medium: 8–24.99 per cent
▶ High: 25–50 per cent
▶ Very high: over 50 per cent

As people have become aware of the dangers of some ingredients in paints – especially VOCs, which are easily smelled – paint manufacturers have been obliged to clean up their manufacturing and processing, and reduce the amount of solvents used. However, a useful measure of the many dangers involved in paint is the Environmental Protection Agency's list of the industries that cause the most pollution – paint factories are still among the heaviest environmental polluters in the USA.

WATER-BASED PAINTS

In developing water-based paints, manufacturers have merely substituted one set of dangerous chemicals for another, including acrylics. In fact, these paints contain more chemicals than the solvent-based types. The solvent replacements are harmful substances such as vinyls, acrylics and acetates. Many dangerous emulsifiers and de-foaming, neutralizing and setting agents are also needed when solvents are reduced. In addition, water-based paints are subject to microbial growth, so preservatives and fungicides such as formic aldehyde and chlorinated hydrocarbons, are used. And most water-borne gloss paints still typically contain 20 per cent solvents. A review

of safety in paints demonstrated that while water-based paints may be low in VOCs, they cannot be considered any healthier than solvent-based paints. During production, water-based paints also give off damaging environmental emissions, particularly carbon dioxide. Titanium dioxide is a widely used ingredient, the processing of which produces sulphuric acid emissions, although recently these have become tightly controlled.

A study published by America's Green Seal organization in 1999 examined 2,200 makes and types of paints and rejected 1,435 of these because they contained dangerous ingredients. The remaining 565 were tested for VOCs and other chemicals and of these, only 71 could be recommended as safe to use. This amounts to only 13 per cent of the paints available. The chemicals listed on p.178 are some of the most common ingredients in paint.

NATURAL ORGANIC PAINTS

No paint is 100 per cent safe. But those that are made entirely from natural ingredients meet many of the criteria for products that are safe for the environment and safe for the home. The vegetable and mineral ingredients used in natural paints are generally from renewable sources and most, but not all, exist in abundance. These paints cause very few toxic emissions, have negligible effects on health and biodegrade safely in land or water.

The traditional disadvantages of natural paints – small batch mixing, variable supplies, uneven coatings, slow drying and lack of durability – have largely been eliminated in modern natural paints. Processes for making these paints sometimes follow the closed-loop, bio-engineering principles that are just beginning to offer benign products in other areas of manufacture (see pp.30–31 and p.168). Pigments and fillers are made from coloured vegetable and mineral extracts. Binders and dispersion elements that replace VOCs are drawn from the natural oils of linseed, safflower, wood, tung, eucalyptus, hemp and orange peel. A common resin is damarra, which comes from the meranti tree; other resins are extracted from larch, pine, mastic and copal trees, and waxes come from the carnauba plant and beehives.

All of these organic finishes contain fewer ingredients than synthetic paints. But they are not totally free of harmful substances. Solvents are still needed, but these are usually derived from vegetable extracts such as orange peel. Cobalt, cadmium and titanium oxides are still in use because substitutes of equal quality have not yet been found. But the most rigorous manufacturers strive to use the least harmful formulation of a substance – for example, one manufacturer uses titanium sulphide rather than the more harmful titanium oxide. Offgassing of natural solvents can be irritants but only during painting and until the paint has cured.

DECORATIVE PERFORMANCE

One of the most significant claims for organic paints is that they have a different visual quality to synthetic paints. Natural colour pigments seem to have a softness that is more pleasing than the 'hard' quality of synthetic paints. The different size of the particles in the paint catch the light differently and their subtle inconsistencies give the surface life and variety. Most organic paints also offer greater vapour permeability which prevents walls sweating or suffering from condensation, avoiding mould and bacterial growth. Synthetic paints, by contrast, do not 'breathe' – although microporous paints are available for external timber decoration.

In terms of performance, there is no evidence that organic coatings are inferior to solvent-borne coatings. Tests have shown that they tend to be marginally more difficult to apply, but they have greater colour stability. No building materials are stable and all paints need to be flexible otherwise they crack. The acrylic in petrochemical paints causes them to become brittle while the natural oils in organic paints perform much better. The only significant disadvantage of organic vegetable-based paints appears to be that they dry more slowly. But this seems a small price to pay for the advantages they offer.

LIMEWASHES AND DISTEMPERS

Limewashes, distempers and caseine paints were commonly used to decorate houses before the introduction of chemical paints. Their subtle, flat colours have come to be so valued that many synthetic paint manufacturers produce paints that aim to match these qualities. All these paints are made from simple ingredients. Lime comes from burnt limestone and although its production demands a great deal of energy, it is an abundant natural resource, and requires no other chemicals. Distemper is also a very basic material, consisting of a suspension of chalk powder mixed with natural binders in water. Caseine is a milk extract that has been an ingredient of paints and glues for centuries. It is mixed with chalk, linseed oil and sometimes egg to make paints that are similar to distempers.

Limewash is probably the most popular of these paints today. Traditionally, limewash required the laborious and messy slaking of quicklime to form lime putty, which then needed to stand for a few days before it could be used. Today, you can buy hydrated lime powder and mix it with powdered pigments to give a range of colours unrivalled by any synthetic paint. It is not, however, as long-lasting as lime putty paints. The impracticalities of limewashing have been exaggerated – it requires no greater skill than painting, although more coats are generally needed. Note that limewash is not suitable for application over existing paints, but caseine paints adhere to almost any surface.

Limewash, distemper and caseine paints generally come in powder form for mixing with water – sometimes the pigments are added separately. Follow the instructions carefully – failure to do so might result in the paints becoming powdery on the wall. This can be avoided by adding more binders such as linseed oil. Take care when mixing limewash – while lime is safe when carbonated (that is, cured by air), it is caustic on the skin. Always wear a mask when mixing any powdered substances.

CHOOSING SAFE PAINTS

If possible, select paints that have the largest number of natural ingredients or those with the lowest VOC content. Be aware that the best quality and safest paint will require careful and patient application – all paints that claim to be 'quick drying' or 'one coat' achieve this convenience with the help of chemical ingredients and should be avoided. Also to be avoided, if at all possible, are paints that contain chlorine or formaldehyde.

In terms of ethical issues, manufacturers of natural paints appear to score highest. The dangers to workers and the devastating pollution associated with some of the large

Natural paints need not be neutral. Here rich, glowing pigments add drama and character to rooms (left and far left).

paint manufacturers are among the worst recorded – evidence of the scant attention they give to ethical issues. By contrast, some of the organic paint manufacturers are paying attention to such issues, attempting, for example, to ensure that the extraction of resins in tropical countries is carried out in such a way as to safeguard the stock of plant resources and create sustainable economies. To minimize transport energy, they try to source vegetable ingredients cultivated close to the factory.

There are so many thousands of paint recipes that it is impossible to grade every type. The following list grades paints by types, from the least to the most dangerous – limewash and distempers are the safest paints of all. The chemicals in paint (listed more fully on p.196) which cause most damage to the environment are generally also those that have the most adverse effect on indoor air quality.

1. Limewash, distemper and caseine
2. Vegetable and mineral paints – water-dispersion types
3. Vegetable and mineral – solvent-dispersion types
4. Synthetic water-based – low-VOC content
5. Synthetic solvent-based – high-VOC content

SAFETY PRECAUTIONS WHEN USING PAINT

▶ Avoid the use of paint where possible. Use natural oils on wood.
▶ Select the safest paint you can find.
▶ For environmental safety as well as appearance, apply paint sparingly.
▶ Reduce amount of paint used by overpainting light colours with dark, rather than the other way round.
▶ Buy only the amount of paint you need to avoid waste.
▶ If using any high-VOC paints or two-part polyurethane coatings, wear a mask of the type recommended by the manufacturer.
▶ Always wear a mask when spray painting, which is particularly dangerous since paint can easily be breathed in. Use a respirator mask – a dust mask is of little value.
▶ When painting or using strippers, keep doors and windows open. If working with solvent-based paints, use an electric fan to help disperse fumes.
▶ Avoid paint strippers that contain dichloromethane, known to be a potent carcinogen. Use a hot air stripper or scrapers instead.
▶ Never throw leftover paint down the drain or into the rubbish. Seal cans tightly to prevent leakage and, if possible, take them to a paint-recycling depot. In the UK there is a network called Community Re-Paint, which arranges to recycle and reuse half-used tins of paint. Otherwise, take leftover paint to an approved chemical waste site, which your local authority should be able to recommend.

STRIPPING PAINT

The desire for greater convenience and speed has driven manufacturers to develop ever fiercer and more aggressive solutions to make paint removal easier and quicker. Prevalent in many paint strippers has been the solvent DCM (dichloromethane), which is a severe skin irritant, and methylene chloride. Both ingredients are carcinogenic.

Water-based, solvent-free strippers are available from manufacturers of natural paints. These give off no fumes and are significantly safer to use. The safest way to strip paint, however, is either with a hot-air stripper or abrasives and scrapers, and a poultice will use fewer chemicals than liquid strippers.

CLEANING BRUSHES

Brushes used with water-based paints can be washed, but only rinse them in running water after most of the paint has been washed away. For brushes used with oil-based paints, select a citrus-solvent brush cleaner. To minimize use of cleaners and water:

▶ Wipe as much paint as possible off brushes before cleaning.

▶ Do most of the washing in a container, thoroughly squeezing out paint from the bristles.

▶ When using brush cleaner, use the same pot for all colours by washing light colours first.

CLEAR WOOD TREATMENTS

Some clear synthetic coatings such as polyurethane varnishes – particularly the two-part systems that require mixing on site – are among the most dangerous of any coatings. Although extremely hard wearing, they include dangerous chemicals such as isocyanates and amine. Transparent stains are particularly high in the solvents or water-dispersal agents discussed above, which enable the stain to penetrate the wood.

To protect wooden surfaces from dirt and abrasion, it is much better to impregnate them with oils and waxes than to paint them with synthetic coatings. The Scandinavians have long known that oils, particularly tung oil, are as good as any synthetic finish, and use of these Scandinavian formulations is growing. Other examples of such natural finishes include boiled linseed oil and oils mixed with

SURFACE PROTECTION
Traditional oils and waxes lend a richness to these boards while protecting the surface.

TRANSLUCENT STAIN
A light stain on these wall and floor-boards gives soft colour but allows the grain to shine through (right).

solvents such as natural turpentine or citrus extracts. Oils and waxes leave the texture and grain of the surface visible, sometimes with the addition of colour tinting, while protecting it. They also breathe particularly well, without any loss in durability, which is essential because wood moves all the time in response to changes in humidity and temperature. Non-hardening oils, such as raw linseed, leave an oily surface that can attract dirt, but some finishes contain natural oils and resins that harden on contact with air. The most beautiful protective indoor treatment for wooden furniture is to saturate it with a natural oil such as boiled linseed or tung oil and then apply a finish of natural wax. Nothing compares with the finish achieved on old furniture over generations of polishing, but the wax does need renewing and polishing at intervals. For floors or work-tops, an application of tung or similar oils is probably the most practical finish.

Organic and low-solvent colour stains, formulated with natural ingredients and spirits, are becoming more common today. Stains for internal use do not need to protect wood from external weathering and can, therefore, be made with few harmful ingredients. Avoid using external stains and preservatives indoors because they have fungicide and anti-microbial ingredients.

GLASS

THE DESIGN OF LARGE WINDOWS FOR ADMITTING LIGHT, so characteristic of modern architecture, went hand in hand with the public health movement that followed the growth of the dark, smoke-filled towns of the Industrial Revolution during the nineteenth century. Early modern architecture, particularly in northern Europe, used the newly available large sheets of float glass to create interiors that were as sunny and light as possible. Today, Scandinavian homes remain exemplars of light, bright modern design. Elsewhere, the importance of creating light-filled interiors continues to grow as we spend more and more time indoors.

Glass can help to create magical interiors, not only by admitting light and sun, but also by linking interiors to the outside world. But glass can also cause problems such as heat loss, overheating through solar gain, and poor sound-proofing. These disadvantages, so prevalent in twentieth-century buildings, can today be eliminated by the careful selection of new, sophisticated types of glass which improve insulation and soundproofing. Glass beams and columns are now being developed that make use of the structural strength of the material.

GLASS PRODUCTION

Glass fulfills many of the criteria for environmentally sound products. High quality glass, known as float glass, however, is produced in only a few large factories world-wide and so is often transported long distances. Glass is made of two-thirds silica sand and one-third mineral compounds such as soda and dolomite, all of which exist in relative abundance.

The main environmental problem associated with glass is the amount of heat needed in its production, which involves large quantities of fossil fuel and consequent polluting emissions. Glass has no adverse affects on indoor health (apart from the risk of breakages – see p.143). It is also safe when disposed of, although very small quantities of chemicals may leach out.

GLASS AND SOLAR GAIN

Unless windows are designed specifically for solar gain, it may be necessary to ensure that they don't cause rooms to overheat when they are struck by the sun. A wide variety of anti-sun glasses, made with coatings and metallic films designed to cut out solar gain, are available.

From an environmental point of view, however, making use of heat gain in winter and using shading devices in summer (see pp.54–57) is far better than using anti-sun glasses. Solar gain is a useful and free source of warmth (p.66), but in order to exploit it without becoming uncomfortable in the summer months, flexible shading devices are usually necessary. These can become attractive decorative elements in their own right. Many of the devices for controlling ventilation, such as slatted and pierced screens, shutters and blinds, show how traditional builders developed simple and effective methods of coping with changes in sun angle and brightness through the year.

THERMAL INSULATION

A priority in any environmentally sound house must be to minimize heat demand and the loss of heat through windows. This can be achieved using a number of products:
▶ Thermal-resisting 'low emessivity' glasses
▶ Double-glazed units
▶ Double-glazed units with argon gas in the void
▶ Secondary windows
The most effective way to increase the insulation value is an air gap between sheets of glass. Even more effective is to fill the space with an inert gas such as argon. An air gap only increases insulation if it is more than 6 mm. Ideally a 12 mm or, even better, 15 mm, air space should be achieved – but this is often difficult in existing windows, unless a special form of double glazing known as a stepped section, with one pane of glass bigger than the other, is tailormade to fit. The most efficient form of glazing is provided by two sheets of high-performance glass filled

with argon. This is twice as effective as two sheets of 6 mm clear glass with a 12 mm air cavity and four times as effective as a single sheet of 6 mm glass. Triple glazing is common in northern countries which have long, icy winters, such as Scandinavia but it is not possible to install in existing windows.

A number of specialist glazing suppliers produce a range of tailormade glazing units that combine different types of glass, offering up to 60 per cent more efficiency than straightforward double-glazed units. But these figures need to be kept in perspective: although the difference in window efficiency can be great, windows in the majority of homes amount to just a small proportion of wall area, so the dwelling's overall efficiency gain will be relatively small. Expensive new glazing may, therefore, not offer the most economical environmental improvement, and other ways of saving heat are likely to be more cost effective (see p.66). Seek guidance from professionals or advisory organizations (see p.192 and pp. 172–89 before embarking on expensive window changes.

Another factor that may affect insulation is the window frame: since the frame can constitute 10–20 per cent of the area of the window, it is important to ensure that it is made of an insulating material. Wood is an excellent insulator. Old metal-framed windows, on the other hand, are highly inefficient. Newer aluminium or steel windows may have what is called a thermal break, in which the cold, outer parts are separated form the inner ones by an insulating core, so that cold is not conducted from the outside to the inside.

GLASS AND NOISE CONTROL

Most of the noise entering a dwelling from outside comes through the windows. Changing the type of glass in a window can considerably reduce the amount of external noise that enters a dwelling – providing that other measures, including blocking air paths through frames, fan openings and so on, are also taken. Sound-reducing glasses available range from specially treated single glass layers to sealed double-glazed units. Double-glazed units designed for thermal insulation will perform extremely well as insulators against noise; unlike thermal insulation there is no optimum width – the greater the width of the cavity the

better. To obtain a good level of sound reduction, however, it is almost certainly more cost effective to add a separate, secondary or inner window than to modify windows to take sealed double-glazed units. By lining the jambs between the inner and outer windows with soft, absorbent material such as thick felt or softboard, even greater noise reduction can be achieved (see table and diagram on p.87 for more information on the degree of sound reduction achieved by different sorts of glass).

GLASS AND SAFETY

Two factors determine how dangerous glass is when it breaks: its strength and resistance to breakage, and the sharpness of the pieces that result on breaking. A number of 'safe' glasses are available, but only two are in fact deemed 'safety glasses' within UK building regulations.

▶ Laminated glass is possibly the safest glass. It is made from two sheets of unstrengthened glass laminated on either side of a transparent film. This creates great impact strength, so when it does break, it will crack but remain intact, which makes it good for security.

▶ Toughened glass is strengthened by annealing after being cut to size. It is very strong and difficult to break. But when it breaks, toughened glass shatters into small, relatively safe pieces.

▶ Wired glass is not a safety glass, but is strengthened by a fine mesh of wires embedded in it, which provides greater strength than ordinary glass. It is not classed as a safety glass because, although strong, it produces sharp spears of glass when it breaks.

▶ Polycarbonate clear sheet is sometimes used as a safe glass substitute: it is virtually unbreakable, but scratches easily and tends to have less clarity than plate glass. It is an unsound petrochemical-derived plastic and should be avoided.

Fire-resistant glasses are also available and in some types of dwellings, such as apartment blocks or houses with more than two floors, it is mandatory to use these for any glass that separates kitchens from staircases and corridors. This is a specialist field and if making any changes to existing glass or if using any glass in these locations, take advice first from your local building inspectorate.

CHANGING LIGHT
Coloured glasses offer constantly changing effects as light conditions vary through the day and year. They are also an ideal way of providing privacy while admitting light.

NOTE

All glass in the home that is at risk of being broken – for example, glass that is lower than 80 cm above the floor, any glass in a door or a glass panel within 30 cm either side of a door – must be certified safety glass. Any clear sheet of glass that people might not see and could walk into should be marked at 1.5 m from the floor to make it visible.

FABRICS

OR STYLE – ADD FABRIC – it can instantly transform a space and create atmosphere. This primary furnishing element has for centuries been used to cover walls, windows, doorways, hard benches, bunks and tables in homes ranging from bare wooden huts to stone castles. The role of fabric in the home used to be so important that in the grandest houses it was the upholsterer who master-minded internal works and employed the cabinet-maker and other interior craftsmen.

Fabric helps to keep the home warm by providing some insulation; it also absorbs sound, creating a 'soft' acoustic, and gives physical comfort. Whether shiny, sparkling, crisp, supple or soft, it carries an array of stylistic messages – all conveyed simply by colour and texture. The gentle earth tones and rough textures of 'natural' fabrics, for example, often suggest a safe, homely comfortable look. But this bears no relation to the environmental or domestic safety of a fabric: that is determined by the extent to which chemicals are used in the process of yarn growing and fabric finishing.

TEXTILE PRODUCTION

Textiles are produced all over the world and are a major commodity in international trade. Their production is linked to the economies of third-world communities – and to those of the first-world global chemical companies who sell these communities vast quantities of chemical fertilizers and pesticides. The chemicals are used to combat the many diseases and pests to which the plants used to make yarn fibre are prone.

So many chemicals are used in the production of cotton, in particular, that the fibre is a major contributor to global environmental degradation and the trade in unhealthy products. While cotton is grown on just 3 per cent of the world's cultivated land, it consumes 25 per cent of world-wide production of chemical fertilizers and pesticides, which include DDT and pyrethroids. Mechanical harvesting of cotton also often involves chemical defoliation.

Chemical-dependent patterns of agriculture have increased because insects have developed resistance to pesticides used, so more and more new products have to be used against them. And chemically fertilized land (as opposed to land fertilized with natural humus) demands ever-increasing chemical use to sustain production. A vicious circle of destruction ensues, with increasing expenditure on costly chemicals accompanied by a decline in production which affects the economies of many third-world communities. Bio-engineered crops create similar patterns of chemical dependency. The same issues are also associated with wool production, which can involve chemicals such as DDT and organophosphates. These have been banned for use on human food crops, but remain as residues on the fabrics that we use in our homes.

PROCESSING FIBRES

The subsequent processing of both vegetable and animal fibres into cloth involves more chemicals, such as chlorine, formaldehyde and polymer coatings, for desizing, scouring, cleaning, bleaching pre-shrinking and other processes. Following this, the cloth is subject to further chemical treatments during mercerizing, dyeing, printing, softening or stiffening and in treatments such as stain-resistance, fireproofing and easy-care. Chemicals residues left by all the finishing and colouring processes can account for up to 20 per cent of the weight of the cloth: you may feel comfortable with a fine cotton sheet next to your skin but, unless it was organically produced, what you probably have is a film of dangerous chemicals. In addition, these processes involve vast quantities of water, which becomes polluted with a variety of chemicals.

Many of the processes described above arise from the consumer demand for certain performance standards in fabrics. We, as consumers, can make a positive contribution to environmental, health and ethical issues by instead demanding fabric that is produced from organically grown yarns, does not involve chemical processes and is coloured

EMBROIDERED DECORATION
Traditional embroidery on cotton
fabrics provides decoration while
avoiding dyes.

with vegetable-based dyes instead of synthetic chemicals. This would break the downward spiral of land degradation and the destruction of yarn-producing communities in the third world. It could also help us to create safe, attractive and satisfying homes with traditional organic fabrics or with new fabrics made using closed-loop production processes (see pp. 30–1).

CHEMICALLY BASED SYNTHETIC FABRICS

Fabrics cannot simply be categorized as manmade or natural, because many yarns and fabrics, such as rayon and acetate, contain blends of natural fibres, natural cellulose and chemical-based filaments. Acrylic, nylon, polyester and nearly all other synthetic yarns, however, are produced almost entirely from petrochemically derived polymers by polluting processes. They are generally less costly to make than the natural fibres they attempt to emulate, and offer supposedly beneficial performance characteristics, such as resistance to moisture, stains, shrinking or crumpling. They may also be lightweight, quick drying and easy to wash. But these synthetic fabrics have the serious environmental problems of linear and dirty industrial processes discussed in chapter one (see pp. 30–1).

Although it is true that some of the early processes needed to transform natural fibre into yarn are not required for synthetic fabrics, many polluting processes are necessary at a later stage. The conversion of the base petrochemical materials into fibres requires them to be either dissolved in solvents or melted, both of which are high-energy, polluting processes. These yarns also need larger amounts of chemicals to colour and wash them than natural fibres do.

The extent of the pollution caused by US synthetic cloth manufacture is demonstrated by the Environmental Protection Agency's list of top polluting industries – two of the three biggest polluters in the USA are manufacturers of synthetic yarns. Emissions from their factories include acetic acid, formaldehyde, solvents, chlorine substances and other dangerous chemicals. Another disadvantage of synthetic fibres is that they can give off toxic fumes in fires. To prevent this happening, some are treated with a variety of dangerous chemical substances, including bromines, halogens and formaldehyde.

SAFE NATURAL FABRICS

The same general environmental principle applies to fabric as to other materials: the less it has been processed, and the nearer it is to its natural state, the safer it will be. Some natural plant fibres, such as linen, flax, hemp, jute and sisal, as well as animal fibres, can be produced with considerably less processing and chemical treatment than cotton. The natural structure of these safe plant fibres consists mainly of cellulose which makes them pliable, absorbent and strong. Each has its own characteristics, requiring certain methods of growing and processing with different environmental and health consequences.

Fibres such as hemp, jute, sisal and ramie offer huge potential to create a wonderfully rich range of furnishing options. They also maintain their original appearance because they stand up well to wear, and when they become waste they will harmlessly biodegrade. Organic fabrics are particularly useful for use in bedding for people suffering chemical or other allergic reactions.

Flax and linen are often confused as they both come from the flax plant. Flax fabric is rougher than linen and is produced during the earlier phases of transforming the fibre into linen. Both are strong, supple and absorbent and have a natural lustre, tending to become more attractive with age. Although flax is a limited crop because it requires fertile land and a maritime climate, it can be easily grown using natural crop protection methods such as soil rotation, rather than chemicals. Retting – the separation of the fibres from the woody plant – is achieved without the use of chemicals by keeping the fibres damp over a period.

Hemp is extremely strong and has long been used for making products such as rope, sacking and sailcloth. Because it is a bark fibre and not a seed fibre like cotton and flax, it grows well without herbicides, fungicides or fertilizers. This makes hemp ideal for the production of non-chemically treated yarns and encourages the use of environmentally safe processes in the later stages.

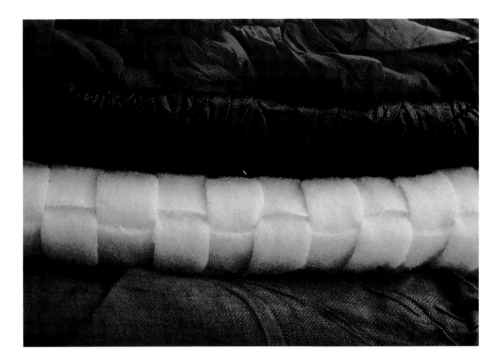

Although the yarn-producing hemp plant is not the same as the marijuana plant, its cultivation is forbidden in the USA. Stocks generally come from China and more recently from eastern Europe.

Ramie is one of the oldest of all fibres and was used to make fabric in ancient China. It has a similar 'natural' appearance to linen but is less costly to produce. Ramie takes dye easily and therefore needs a minimum of chemical additives for colour-fast dyeing. It is absorbent like cotton, dries quickly, and is resistant to bacteria and moulds, so needs no treatment. It has a high lustre but is rather rough, so it is often combined with other fabrics for softness. Its resistance to abrasion makes it an excellent fabric to use for upholstery.

Wool has many unique qualities that have long been recognized and it is only recently that chemicals have been used in its processing. It makes beautiful fabric that needs little enhancing and is naturally strong and resilient for its weight. It is also highly insulating, contains natural stain-resistant oils such as lanolin and is self extinguishing in fires. Untreated wool can absorb up to a third of its own weight in water before feeling wet to the touch.

Organic cotton can be produced without chemical treatment. There is a proprietary range of cottons called FoxFibre, which are made from organically grown cotton plants that have been bred to be self coloured and require no dyes. Self-coloured cottons have always existed, but their short fibres were suited only to hand production. Sally Fox of FoxFibre in California used natural breeding processes to develop fibre lengths suitable for mechanized manufacture, thus making these natural yarns a commercial proposition. They come in a range of natural earth tones – rust, cream, browns and greens – and new colours are being developed.

In design terms, one of the great assets of these natural textiles is that the colours become more intense the more they are washed. The cost of undyed organic fabrics like these is still high – production quantities are so small they cannot compete with mass-produced cotton – but weight for weight they use approximately 30 per cent less in resources.

SAFE MANMADE FABRICS

New manmade fabrics are being developed for production by sustainable, clean methods, including the use of recycled materials. Lyocell, usually known by its trade names Tencel™ and Cupro™, is a wholly manmade fabric, said to be the only significant 'new' fibre developed in many

NEW CLEAN PROCESSES
A fabric made by the ground-breaking DesignTex™ company, using clean processes (above). Only safe chemicals are used.

NATURAL COLOURS
This multicoloured Ikat fabric is beautiful and safe. It is made with natural dyes and vegetable-based colourings (above).

years. It derives entirely from natural woodpulp cellulose, without any toxic or polluting chemicals, and the majority of the processing agents are recyclable. It takes colour well, is absorbent and strong when wet, drapes well and biodegrades easily.

Other new fabrics, such as the Climatex Lifecycle™ products, set a high standard in clean production. This pioneering fabric from DesignTex is made from worsted wool and ramie and the production exemplifies new safe processes (see p.31).

Another type of environmentally positive fabric is made from recycled thermoplastic components. The USA alone discards 2.5 million drinks bottles made from PET (poly-ethelyene teraphthalate) every hour! This inert waste is ground up to form the base ingredient for fabric filaments – although dyeing these fibres may have the same impact as the dyeing of petrochemical fibres. The recycling process requires low energy because the temperatures need not be high, therefore the release of emissions is low. Transport of waste is an environmental cost, but the problems of waste is so great that any such attempt at using it deserves to be supported. Recycled PET fabric is best known for fleece garments, but is also used for making warm bed covers as well as carpet.

COLOURING AND PRINTING

The addition of colour to fabric and the creation of prints and patterns are among our most rewarding decorative traditions. For centuries, naturally occurring vegetable, animal and mineral dye compounds were used to colour fabric, but today synthetic dyes are used, adding to the environmental damage caused by chemical-based fabric cultivation and processing. Dyeing and rinsing processes for colouring fabric alone generate 65 litres of waste water for every 500 grams of fabric product. The average USA dyeing facility generates between one and two million gallons of waste water per day!

Fabrics that are considered safe are either left as their natural colour or are dyed using age-old recipes for naturally occurring dyes. This need not limit the range of colours available, as demonstrated by the sumptuous cloths made prior to the introduction of synthetic dyes in the nineteenth century. All used natural dyes – although admittedly some of the strongest colours contained heavy metals such as chrome, nickel, cadmium and cobalt. Naturally dyed fabrics that are easily the equal of any synthetic dyes are available today.

STAIN-RESISTANCE TREATMENTS

Fabrics are commonly treated with chemicals to increase their resistance to stains, but the safety of these treatments has recently come into question. One of the most common treatments, a worldwide market leader, has recently been withdrawn from the UK market because it uses PFO (perfluorocatanyl sulphate), a chemical that enters human tissue and is understood to be carcinogenic. Research has shown that the only human blood found to be free of this product is in samples taken prior to the invention of PFO. The Environmental Protection Agency in the USA is urging a worldwide ban on this common but deadly chemical. Moth proofing, too, uses contact insecticides that should be avoided and fire-proofing treatments involve a range of dangerous chemicals.

CERTIFICATION OF FABRICS

Because the dangers of such extensive use of chemicals on fabrics has been recognized, the certification of fabrics is more widespread than it is for many materials. A number of organizations offer labelling systems to certify that a fabric is safe. Some of the best known of these organizations and their logos are listed on pp.194–5. The criteria they assess are not entirely consistent, but cover similar issues: environmental impact or ethical animal breeding during cultivation and the avoidance of chemical finishes, synthetic dyes, heavy metals, residual pesticides and formaldehyde during manufacturing. They also consider ethical issues of employment that may arise during the production process.

PURE COTTON?

Ordinary cotton is treated with many chemicals as it goes through the processes from plant to fabric, and residues remain, even after washing. Choose organic cotton for your bed linen if you want to be sure that you are not breathing in potentially harmful chemicals as you sleep.

COTTON PROCESSING

The chart opposite lists some of the main processes involved in the production of cotton fabric during which an enormous number of chemicals are used. Many other fabrics undergo similar, though less elaborate, processing. By comparison, it is clear that organically produced cotton involves far fewer processes and chemicals and therefore has fewer adverse consequences for both global and domestic environments.

	CHEMICALS USED	GLOBAL CONSEQUENCES	HEALTH CONSEQUENCES	ORGANIC COTTON
COTTON				
CULTIVATION	▶ Synthetic chemical pesticides and fertilizers that may be highly toxic and cause environmental problems	▶ Chemicals cause decline in soil fertility and erosion. ▶ Aerial spraying affects other crops ▶ High water use and water supplies polluted	▶ Traces of chemicals remain and are potentially carcinogenic	▶ **Organic matter fertilizes soil and renews soil productivity** ▶ **Less water used**
HARVESTING	▶ Herbicides used to defoliate and make picking easier	▶ Chemicals pollute ground and rivers ▶ Harvesting machinery compacts the ground and reduces soil productivity	▶ Traces of chemicals remain and are potentially carcinogenic	▶ **Hand picked (no defoliation, machinery or chemicals)** ▶ **Hand picking means less wastage**
SCOURING, WASHING AND BLEACHING	▶ Chlorine, hydrogen peroxide, APEO (alkylphenoloxylate), EDTA (ethylenediamine tetra-acetate) and VOCs	▶ Synthetic disinfectants are slow to biodegrade ▶ Chlorine emissions pollute atmosphere	▶ Traces of chemicals are carcinogenic and can affect the nervous system	▶ **Natural spinning oils biodegrade easily** ▶ **Natural processing such as potato starch used** ▶ **No chlorine used**
YARN DYEING	▶ Compounds of iron, tin, potassium, and VOCs	▶ Large quantities of water used for washing out dyes. ▶ Water polluted by heavy metals	▶ Toxic residues remain	▶ **Natural vegetable dyes or low-impact synthetic dyes or cotton is colour grown**
PRINTING	▶ Solvent-based inks containing heavy metals, benzene and organochlorides	▶ Waste water is polluted with heavy metals ▶ Emissions form harmful ozone	▶ Toxic residues cause problems of the central nervous system, respiratory system and skin, as well as headaches, dizziness and eye irritations	▶ **Natural vegetable and mineral inks and binders are used**
FINISHING: easycare, stain resistance, fire proofing, moth proofing, softening, deodorizing, anti-static, mercerizing	▶ Formaldehyde, caustic soda, sulphuric acid, bromines and urea resins, sulphonamides, halogens and bromines	▶ Waste water has a high acid content ▶ Emissions to atmosphere	▶ Chemical traces on the fabric can cause burning eyes, nose and throat, as well as difficulties with sleep, concentration and memory. Can increase susceptibility to cancer. ▶ Emissions of chemicals from fabric increase with temperature	▶ **No enhancement finishes used**
TRANSPORT In addition to the above are the environmental consequences of transporting huge quantities of chemicals from the area of their manufacture to the place of cultivation, as well as the additional journeys involved for all stages of cotton production, from the raw material to place of manufacture, finishing and then to distributor and user				▶ **Fewer processes so fewer journeys**

FURNITURE

WHEN BUYING FURNITURE, REMEMBER THE '3Rs' and reduce, repair and recycle as much as possible (see p.17). Avoid simply filling space and make sure every piece of furniture fulfills a function. A home free of unnecessary things will appear more spacious, lighter and generally calmer – and will be easier to clean.

There is such a wide range of furniture styles on the market today that avoiding furniture which causes environmental pollution in its production or damages indoor air quality does not mean a limited choice or having to settle for a 'rustic' style. As with so much else, we now have the option of following older, benign traditions or choosing items made by new, clean production methods. Many of the materials from which furniture is made – wood, fabric, plastic, adhesives and finishes – are dealt with elsewhere in this book, but there are a number of aspects discussed in this section that are specific to furniture.

TRADITIONAL BENIGN FURNITURE

Traditional benign furniture used natural materials in simple, economic and efficient ways. This approach has produced some of the world's finest furniture – from

SIMPLE ELEGANCE
This simple, elegant furniture, designed by Alvar Aalto in Finland in the 1930s, combines natural bent beech with canvas fabric (left).

SHAKER STYLE
Like the Aalto examples, Shaker furniture (right) makes the most of natural materials and shapes.

SCULPTURAL FURNITURE

Sculptor Alison Crowther carved this stool from a block of locally grown wood (below). A simple but strikingly beautiful object, it relies on simplicity and the natural colour and texture of the wood grain for its effect.

MODERN RECYCLED MATERIALS

Metamorf Design have explored ways of moulding recycled thermoplastic material in these colourful children's chairs (below). The result is both highly practical, safe and fun.

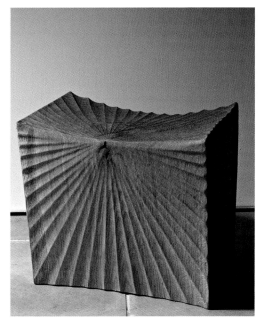

MODERN CRAFTSMANSHIP

This elegant, comfortable dining chair is made by the company Trannon, who use local timber and traditional craftsmanship (above).

primitive items to the more sophisticated simplicity of Shaker furniture – and is still equally valid today.

Solid timber furniture is undergoing a renaissance, with designers developing models based on traditional methods as well as the newer, safe techniques of production. Traditionally, the furniture industry relied on the sustained productivity of woodlands achieved by means of a system known as coppicing, which encourages regeneration. Coppicing involves cutting a young tree, with a trunk of about 10 cm in diameter, just above ground level, leaving the roots intact. Some 15 years later, new trees have grown from those roots, thus enabling one plant to continue producing usable timber for hundreds of years.

Contemporary makers increasingly use coppiced timber to produce furniture that is spare and light. Long, flexible stakes of willow and ash thinnings can also be woven or bent to create interesting forms for chairs, screens and stools. Other designers exploit the powerful look of large pieces of unadorned timber to make chunky tables and

stools – sometimes boldly plain, sometimes with delicate surface carvings and softened shapes. Sculptors are also producing carved furniture from huge sections of wood, using the African carving tradition in which a whole item, legs included, is carved from one trunk. This method avoids glues and joints, but does produce waste. All these designs embody the 'less is more' approach and derive their beauty from a simplicity of line and the richness and texture of the wood grain.

When buying timber furniture, check that the timber is certified as ecologically sound: some retailers advertise these product lines as a marketing aid. In particular, look for products certified by the Forestry Stewardship Council (FSC), which can be relied upon to be safe. Even better, select only materials and products that originate locally, thereby avoiding large transport costs. And remember that the finish on any furniture is just as important as the materials, so check that finishes and jointing glues are non toxic (for more information see p.196).

Rattan is a renewable material. It is handcrafted to make items such as this chair which is comfortable and ecologically sound (left).

This unusual chair is covered with a material made of safe woven grass (below).

Furniture is also being made from many other natural materials such as rushes, rattan and bamboo. Bamboo is one of the fastest-growing renewable resources and is also extremely strong and durable. It can be combined with plywood in a composite material for making larger pieces such as table tops and worksurfaces. Another traditional safe material now being used for interesting designs is made from wood-based paper twine woven into a flexible fabric – sometimes incorporating wire for extra strength – and stretched over a bentwood or cane frame. Such furniture has long been used in the tropics but is now becoming universally popular.

RECYCLED FURNITURE AND WASTE MATERIALS

Buying new furniture is not the only way to furnish your home. Many attractive and stylish homes contain long-lasting furniture that has been used before – whether 'antique' or simply secondhand. This approach allows you to select items without constraints of style or period,

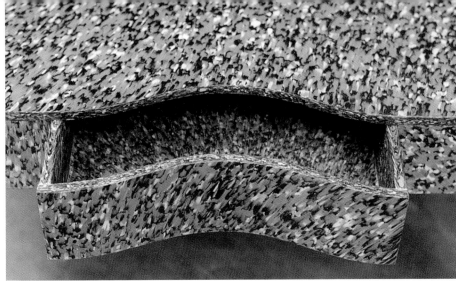

RECYCLED PLASTIC

This table top and drawer are made from recycled thermoplastic material such as drinks bottles (above). Like traditional plastic, this material is strong, practical and easy to clean.

A NEW LOOK

This desk by the Californian company Studio eg is made entirely from recycled materials (right). The top is recycled plastic, the legs are made from recycled paper tube and the feet of recycled rubber. The floor tiles are also made of recycled plastic drink bottles.

basing your choice on merit alone. Tables, chairs, wardrobes, kitchen units, bathroom fittings, door handles and windows – anything you can imagine – can be sourced through salvage centres or secondhand shops. Furnishing in this way demands fewer new products, so consumes fewer resources and creates less waste.

The recycling of waste to make new materials is the foundation of nature's processes. By incorporating this principle into manufacturing processes, we can both cope with waste and create materials without consuming more resources. In the USA, reuse of waste is now a significant industry that produces a wide range of materials for making contemporary furniture. Materials being reprocessed include plastic bottles, car tyres, waste roofing materials, glass and aluminium. Agricultural waste, such as straw, rice and flax, and safe glues can be used to make sheet materials to replace unsafe woodchip boards. Strong panels for furniture are made with light, honeycomb cores in a variety of materials, including recycled aluminium. Paper pulp is an ideal material for smaller items, such as lamp shades, and recycled paper in tube form is being used for legs of tables and desks.

NEW MATERIALS

Petrochemical plastics have many advantages: they are cheap, solid, durable, easily moulded and formed, and require no surface finishing. But they are a danger to the environment and our homes. Two new types of plastic with the same practical advantages are beginning to replace the petrochemical plastics: one is made by recycling of thermoplastic waste such as plastic bottles; the other uses plant fibres suitable for processing into plastic substitute.

The first type of new plastic is made from discarded drinks bottles which are shredded, then washed and heat-formed into moulds or flat sheets. Depending on the process, the waste is either homogenized into a material of a dark charcoal colour, or the colours of the original waste remain to give a multi-coloured, flecked appearance. This new plastic has all the advantages of traditional plastic surfaces and laminates and can be used as flat panels or bent into 'organic' forms. In the USA, a range of office furniture made from recycled plastic and other recycled materials is available and should soon enter the domestic market. One range of recycled plastic has been certified safe for use with food so is ideal for kitchen worktops.

The second way of making plastic without petro-chemicals makes use of vegetable substances as a base. To date, developments with hemp fibre are giving the best results – it grows well and its long, strong fibres are ideal for processing. There are no polluting emissions and the resource is renewable and biodegradable. Farmers in the UK have been growing hemp for use in car body parts and an Austrian company has developed a hemp-based plastic for moulding into a variety of objects such as computer cases, handles and doorknobs. Growing awareness of the need for more environmentally sound materials should soon bring these materials into the furniture industry

ALUMINIUM AND METAL FURNITURE

Metal components are used in furniture to provide strength and durability. All metals come from finite resources and consume energy in production, but more and more metals are being recycled. For example, most aluminium used today has been recycled. While aluminium demands very high-energy input when processed from mined natural bauxite, it lends itself easily to recycling, which uses only 10 per cent of the original energy and causes fewer emissions than the original production. The production of primary steel consumes less energy than aluminium, but more energy is needed to recycle the metal. Most steel in furniture and appliances contains about 50 per cent recycled material.

Refinishing treatments can be costly. While recycled aluminium can be left without a surface finish, recycled steel needs to be coated and many of the most durable

coatings such as chroming and galvanizing use polluting heavy metals. In addition, paints used on steel are often solvent- or polymer-based, which may be harmful (see p.135). The growth in the reuse of materials means that the environmental consequences of recycling are as important as those associated with primary production. Recycling processes are now being designed to ensure that they create much less environmental damage.

AIR-FILLED FURNITURE

Perhaps the cleanest and safest, most environmentally friendly furniture of all is that made of air. Recently available is a range of air-filled chairs and sofas which are a far cry from the uncomfortable, inflatable PVC bubble furniture of the 1970s. The furniture is ergonomically shaped and retains its form because it is made of separate air-filled sections of plastic material. The plastic is so strong that the supplier guarantees the replacement of any part that may be punctured, free of charge. The inflated item is covered with a comfortable slip case made in one of a range of materials. While the plastic is not benign, it is 100 per cent recyclable and the environmental advantages of using so little material to create such a large item are clear – a good example of less is best.

MASS-PRODUCED PANEL FURNITURE

When labour was cheap and demand could be satisfied by small-scale workshops, furniture of every design was made by craftsmen using safe methods and local timber. But mass-production factories aimed to reduce labour costs, and new fabrication techniques and materials made this possible. Using thin wood veneers, particles and waste chips, sheet materials such as plywood, particle-board, chipboard and medium-density fibre-boards, were developed. Desks, wardrobes, chests and kitchen cabinets, are today assembled from a number of panels of these

engineered boards and finished with factory-applied plastic laminate or paint coatings.

While the use of waste timber chippings and particles is environmentally sound, these materials are usually bonded using adhesives containing formaldehyde and urea resins, which are far from safe. Mass produced in great quantities throughout the world, engineered-board furniture is a danger to the atmosphere during its manufacture and affects indoor air quality through offgassing. It is far less durable than items made of solid wood and is thrown away after a relatively short life, possibly giving off polluting emissions as it degrades.

Another characteristic of panel furniture that is environmentally unsound is its smooth, hard-wearing surface. Such surfaces are achieved by extensive processing, and are usually finished with high-solvent, plastic-based paints. These processes include gluing plastic laminates under heat with dangerous adhesives, the use of fillers and bleaches, and the spray application of heavy-duty petrochemical paints, transparent stains or inks. Acetone, ammonia, hydrogen peroxide as well as very high concentrations of VOCs are commonly emitted during production. In addition, panel furniture is offered in a wide range of colours. Every time a colour is changed, a huge machine clean-up operation is required that uses and pollutes large quantities of water.

Panels of engineered board are normally thin (12–19 mm) and the fixings and joints are weak. This means that if the fixings break, the panel is damaged and little can be done by way of repair. Furthermore, these materials are particularly prone to damage when wet, although stronger water-resistant types are now becoming available. Hence, countless items such as kitchen units are thrown away, only to be replaced by more particle-board cabinets which differ only in style.

The many disadvantages of panel furniture have been recognized and the manufacturing processes are now being redesigned to adsorb or incinerate the emissions. Replacements are being found for formaldehyde and similar unhealthy compounds. Nevertheless, with the bulk of these materials, the worst problems remain.

INDOOR AIR QUALITY

Panel furniture contains resin glues and polymer surface coatings that contribute to poor indoor air. For the first six months of their lives, such items offgas significantly, and continue to do so for up to 18 months until they become safe. Dampness, abrasion and general wear and tear will exacerbate the level of offgassing.

The only way to avoid formaldehyde offgassing is to coat the board with a sealer but, according to the Environmental Protection Agency, this is only effective if

all surfaces are completely sealed, since gases can travel through the material and exit where the coating is missing. To be sure that all surfaces are sealed you would have to take the furniture apart – generally an impossible task – so as to reach every edge.

Upholstered furniture and beds can harbour dust mites and particulates which have adverse affects on health, and the fabric can also contain toxic residues. It is healthier to select furniture that is not upholstered or has loose tie-on pads that can be removed for regular washing. Avoid upholstery fillings made of any foamed plastic materials as these are likely to offgas.

It is particularly important to bear these issues in mind when choosing beds and bedding.

▶ Choose a good solid wooden frame bed put together with non-toxic glues and finished with organic coatings.

▶ Look for a chemical-free mattress made from organic fabric padding and box springs or natural rubber latex. Natural latex is a renewable safe material and will not harbour dust mites or particulates.

▶ Choose mattress covers, sheets, pillow cases, duvets and duvet covers made of chemical-free cottons or barrier fabrics. These are safe, synthetic fabrics that are so tightly woven that they prevent dust mites getting in but are still air permeable.

Allergy sufferers may find it useful to obtain skin-testing kits from specialist fabric suppliers: these contain all the chemicals used in their manufacture and allow you to test your sensitivity to their product.

FIRE-PROOFED FURNITURE

Some countries legislate that certain articles of furniture – usually foam-filled and fabric-covered items – should be fire proofed. In the UK and USA, all fire-proofed furniture is identified with a label. Fire proofing is generally achieved by coatings of compounds of bromine, as well as formaldehyde, halogens and the sulphides of ammonium, zinc and magnesium, all of which are considered hazardous to health. Ideally, avoid fire-proofed items. Choose furniture that does not easily catch fire, and if it should, does not give off dangerous fumes. In many house fires, injury and death are caused not by the fire itself, but by inhalation of chemical gases released from plastic foams used in upholstered chairs and sofas. Natural materials such as wood and natural fabrics do not pose chemical risk from fire. Wood does not burn easily, but fabrics and paper will be the first items to catch light in a domestic fire.

For this reason one of the largest, most popular retailers and manufacturers of domestic furniture worldwide has adopted the policy of not fire proofing furniture except where legislation makes it obligatory. The best way to make your home safe from fires is to be vigilant and ensure that electric bar heaters and naked flames from candles and fires are guarded and cannot come into contact with fabrics or paper, even if they fall. Every home should be fitted with smoke- or heat-detecting alarms of a type recommended by your local building inspectorate.

1. Only sustainable timbers considered

2. Depends also on distance transported from source to user

3. Depends on finish

4. A high proportion of aluminium is now recycled

✔ GOOD RATING ○ MEDIUM RATING ✘ POOR RATING	RESOURCE DEPLETION	EMBODIED ENERGY [2]	EMISSIONS DURING MANUFACTURE	EFFECT ON INDOOR AIR	CAPACITY FOR RECYCLING/ BIODEGRADING
RE-USED FURNITURE [3]	✔	✔	✔	✔	✔
TIMBER [1,3]	✔	✔	✔	✔	✔
PARTICLE BOARDS	✔	○	✘	✘	✘
STEEL	○	✘	✘	✔	○
ALUMINIUM [4]	✘	✘	✘	✔	✔
PETROCHEMICAL PLASTICS	✘	✘	✘	✘	✘
RECYCLED PLASTICS	✔	○	○	○	✔
NON-ORGANIC NATURAL FABRIC	○	✘	✘	○	○
ORGANIC FABRIC	✔	✔	✔	✔	✔
SYNTHETIC FABRIC	✘	✘	✘	○	○
NEW VEGETABLE FIBRES/PLASTICS	✔	○	✔	✔	✔
BAMBOO [3]	✔	✔	✔	✔	✔

FURNITURE TO LOOK FOR:

▶ Well-made, long-lasting furniture from local materials that can be repaired if necessary.

▶ Furniture made with naturally occurring materials. These biodegrade safely, unlike petrochemical-based plastics, coatings and alloys.

▶ Furniture made from certified timbers.

▶ Furniture made with timber or metal frames. It is much easier to repair than plastic or panel furniture.

▶ Materials that are solid right through, finished with traditional oils and waxes that can be renewed at home and improve with age and use.

▶ Used furniture or furniture made from recycled materials.

▶ Soft furnishings that can be removed for washing.

▶ Organic fabrics and natural padding and fillings.

FURNITURE TO AVOID:

▶ Laminated finishes that are super-smooth; these will become damaged and look worse over time.

▶ Particle or composite boards that include urea or formaldehyde glues.

▶ Furniture made from tropical hardwoods or old-growth temperate hardwoods.

▶ Finishes that are high in VOCs (volatile organic compounds) and other chemicals.

▶ PVC, nylon and other petroleum-based plastics.

▶ Foam- and plastic-filled furniture.

▶ Upholstered furniture.

▶ Fire-proofing that contains bromines, halogens or formaldehyde.

▶ Stain-resistance treatments containing fluorocarbons, PFOs or formaldehyde.

▶ Metal coatings that include chrome, lead or nickel.

RECYCLING

RECYCLING IS ONE OF THE MOST CONSTRUCTIVE WAYS TO be environmentally safe – provided that the process does not demand so much energy through collection and reprocessing that it cancels any benefits. By recycling – and repairing or reusing – we consume fewer resources and less energy, and generate less waste, thereby reducing our impact on the environment.

Recycling is not a new concept. Generations before us have cherished and repaired things used by their parents and grandparents. Recycling was also common practice in building until the twentieth century, when labour became more expensive than materials. This made replacement cheaper than repair but ignored the cost to the earth. Today, a 'newer is better' ethos prevails. But, ironically, the more new things we buy in pursuit of a supposedly better life, the worse we make the world we live in. Some of the consequences of this 'newer is better' ethos have been outlined in chapter one.

The practice of saving resources through reuse – like so much environmental wisdom – can be found in the design traditions of cultures from all over the world. From a design perspective, what is so striking when looking at these traditions are the imaginative leaps that make creativity with reused materials possible. Like all the most creative ideas, they appear obvious, and are often very simple. Examples from traditional cultures are endless – from the reuse, over generations, of timber, stone and brick from buildings; of flattened tin drums to make metal roofing or wall siding; and of copper printing plates on floors. Indigenous peoples have made floors from seashells mixed with lime or fruit stones mixed with blood and dung, while horsehair, dung and even blood have been combined with lime to plaster and colour walls.

The presence of reused materials can create a strong and enjoyable aesthetic – as anyone who has visited ancient Italian or Greek cities where history lives on in walls made of ancient stones, door surrounds of marble columns, steps built of old beams, knows. In a more modest way,

interiors have this same sense of history when paved with reclaimed stones or built with reused timber or brick. In recent years, the realization that nineteenth- and early twentieth-century buildings have period details that warrant saving for reuse – flooring flagstones and old boards, brick, fireplaces, doors, windows and craftsman-produced objects such as decorative mouldings – has given rise to commercial enterprises that salvage and resell these objects. Indeed, they are so sought after that a strange inversion of value has developed: older things, which require no new processing or materials, can be more expensive than the new article. New elements are not in fact cheaper – they are so only because the real costs, the costs to the earth – are not factored in to the cost of their production. But this is changing, and environmental concerns and the merits of recycling are today beginning to be taken seriously – albeit not quickly enough.

RECYCLING TODAY

Households in Britain currently produce 25 million tonnes of waste – expected to double over next 20 years – of which only eight per cent is recycled. In contrast, the Swiss recycle more than 50 per cent of their waste. But it is possible to change the way we think about waste. This is being demonstrated by a few far-sighted members of the industrial community, who are beginning to factor into their accounting the true costs of resource depletion, waste and pollution. More and more products are being manufactured in such a way that they can be easily disassembled for renovation and reuse, and manufacturers are recycling waste for their own production processes. It is important to note here that PVC is wholly unsuitable for

RECYCLED STAIRS
Found metal components, bits of machinery and slabs of recycled timber make for a unique, sculptural staircase.

RECYCLED CANS
Imaginative design has turned old
soft drinks cans into an interesting
door curtain (left).

recycling, despite manufacturers' claims to the contrary. (For more information on PVC, see p.122)

Significant social benefits can arise from recycling. Local skills and small businesses in any community have always benefited from the repair and reuse of artefacts. This is not false idealization of past craftsman-based cultures: it works today in large-scale, commercial economies. In the USA, for example, recycling generates significant employment and revenue for many tens of thousands of firms and the number is growing annually.

There are two main messages for the householder: first, recycling is environmentally safe, and second, the more recycled, environmentally benign products consumers demand, the more manufacturers will offer. Amory Lovins of the Rocky Mountain Institute, the groundbreaking environmental research centre, puts it succinctly: 'It's remarkable how quickly the phrase, "Sorry, we don't make that" changes to, "When do you want it," when the demand is great enough.'

RECYCLING IN THE HOME

A good proportion of the items for any interior can be made from recycled materials and components, which can take a number of forms:

▶ Reused materials – for example, timber, tiles and stone.
▶ Reused building components – for example, windows, doors, taps, bathroom fittings and fireplaces.
▶ Non-traditional materials – for example. straw, newspaper and salvaged components.
▶ Waste items used in different contexts – for example, bottles for walls, cans for curtains or walls, packing cases or pallets for furniture and cable drums for tables. (When using waste materials, it is important to

REUSED TILES
Broken tiles can be used to make
an individual wall covering – but be
sure to use safe adhesives (left).

MAKING GOOD

Repairing household fittings not only extends their life but also helps to save resources (right).

avoid those, such as some timbers, that may have been previously treated with harmful chemicals or preservative sprays.)

▶ Composting kitchen waste, wood shavings, wood ash and similar biodegradable items can greatly reduce the amount of waste that goes to landfill sites. And the resulting compost is good for your garden.

Before you buy anything new, think about whether it can be disassembled and easily repaired. Select products that have been sturdily made, and choose materials that maintain their good appearance and don't 'ugly out', so that you do not have to throw things away simply because they look worse for wear. Although selecting the best may be more expensive in the short term, it will be more economical in the long run. Caring for the environment is precisely not about short-term cost, but about long-term saving. If your budget is limited, think quality rather than quantity. A few fine objects in a room will look far more stylish than lots of inferior furniture.

Before throwing something away, ask yourself if it can be repaired, or whether it can be used, partly or wholly, in some other way, or for some other function. A broken wooden chair, for example, can be repaired by the local carpenter or a steel table leg by a local ironworker. Certain 'natural' materials lend themselves to repair and this can greatly extend their useful lives. Timber, stone and ceramic tiles or bricks develop a recognizable and attractive patina that can be very alluring and this is what makes old houses, interiors, furniture and fittings so special. They accommodate wear and tear over time – a characteristic that many modern materials do not possess.

A whole world of imaginative and interesting design opportunities opens up when you look at objects and

MAKING GOOD

Repairing household fittings not only extends their life but also helps to save resources (right).

RECYCLED SHELVES

These shelves are made of recycled glass. The slight imperfections are part of their charm (right).

PATCHWORK QUILT

Fabric scraps are made into something special by the art of quilting (below).

BARE BRICK

Reused bricks have a pleasing quality and texture that needs no additional covering (right).

OLD TILES

Ceramic tiles can be used time and time again, the patina of age only adding to their attraction (above).

materials around you with a fresh eye to see how they can be used in new ways. No idea should be dismissed, however zany – after all, tractor seat stools and drums of washing machines are now design icons. Other ideas include using wooden crates for shelving systems and old railway sleepers, discarded pallets or even bicycle parts for furniture. Old furniture can also be used in new ways – for example, old cupboards, desk or dresser units can be modified for assembly into kitchen units and worktops. Make chandelier lamps or mobiles from old compact discs, or fashion partitions from old books within a timber framework. Walls can be decorated with newspapers, maps and pages from books or even patchworks of old clothes. The attraction of this way of decorating is that it will create totally individual and personal homes that transcend interior design to become almost sculptural interiors unique to their owners. There can be no better way of saving resources.

But designing with cast-offs needs care, in order to prevent your space from looking like a chaotic assembly of what you happen to have found. The beautiful quilts of New England demonstrate the key to making a beautiful whole from many disparate elements – a strong design discipline organizes the many scraps into a whole. Far from being a limitation, an ordered approach will be a springboard for creativity and ingenuity. For example, when reusing floorboards from different sources or of inadequate lengths, turn this to design advantage by using the boards in a herringbone pattern, or form a pattern of short boards laid crossways within a grid of long boards. Even if you lay boards lengthways as normal there is no need to have consistent board widths or lengths – equal boards derive from mass manufacture and a need for speed in laying. Some of the finest traditional floors are made from random widths and lengths.

Similarly, when using recycled windows or similar components of different sizes, you may be happy with the haphazard 'gypsy' look, or you can organize them by arranging them into a regular grid or framework, again enjoying the interplay of regular and irregular patterns.

The same approach can be used when recycling tiles for floors or walls, where an overall ordering geometry is also important. You can create attractive borders or patterns

NEW MATERIALS

Exploring new materials made from waste can offer exciting opportunities for designers. This comfortable armchair designed by Lothar Windels is made from waste wool recycled into thick felt material (above). Over time the felt gradually adjusts to fit the shape of the body.

using different types of tiles, or even made from broken pieces. Combine large areas of plain concrete or cement screed on floors, or wall plaster, with patterns of broken tiles or glass. The Spanish architect Gaudi and the sculptor Andrew Logan have created sumptuous designs for walls and furniture using broken tiles, glass and mirror work. Developing such designs will give your home a personality unlike any other and look infinitely more delightful than even the most expensive new surface covering.

NEW MATERIALS AND CLEAN PRODUCTION

In the past, many practical devices were made by hand from wood, clay or other naturally occurring materials. This is no longer the case for so much of what we use today. But it is in fact in this sphere of mass production that we are now on a threshold of opportunity for large-scale recycling. The growth of closed-loop processes, or bio-mimicry (see pp. 30–1), offers the potential to develop the most advanced materials, avoiding the environmental damage of dirty industrial processes (see pp. 30–1). Companies such as Interface and Milliken – both carpet companies – IBM, Sony, Gramme GMBH and BMW in

RECYCLED KITCHEN

A discarded iron grill from a London underground station has been rescued to make a hanging pot rack (above). Nearly all of this kitchen, designed by architect Pedro Guedes, has been made from recycled wood, stone and iron.

'ANNIE' CHAIR

'ANNIE' CHAIR

Reestore takes everyday waste objects and cheekily turns them into charming yet functional pieces of furniture and accessories.

INTEGRAL PATTERNS

Careful sorting of the materials used to make recycled plastic sheet can create interesting patterns (below).

Germany, are moving towards being able to supply new products made almost entirely from waste and recycled materials or materials from new 'clean' processes. This applies to technologically sophisticated items such as cars and computers, as well as to more basic items such as engineered boards for floors, and furniture, fabrics and paints. Designers and makers everywhere are marketing stunning ranges of furniture made from recycled plastic; an attractive range of artificial fibre fleece throws are made from plastic drinks bottles; a Spanish company is developing exquisite chairs using waste almond shells, and crushed light bulbs and waste mussel shells are being used to make floor and wall tiles.

Previously unexploited materials from vegetable sources are also coming into use. Hemp, for example, is now recognized as offering enormous potential, not only for fabric fibres but also for making plastic-like substances (see p.157). Of particular interest to designers and decorators are new, sustainable, timber-like products such as bamboo (see p.115). Programmes are under way to find uses for the vast numbers of palms that are cultivated throughout the world for their fruit but have a relatively

NEW AND OLD

This interior combines older reused furniture with modern items such as a hardwood bench and aluminium lights.

short productive life. Coconut palm wood, for example, is proving to be a useful and durable alternative to timber, but inadequate marketing has limited its availability. Newly under consideration is material from the pejibella and concha fruiting palms that grow in Central America. This beautiful material is ebony coloured with light flashes, and is exceptionally durable and tough. Such materials offer interesting and unique design possibilities that are also environmentally safe. While they are not yet readily available, you should look out for them as their availability will grow and they offer exciting possibilities. Consider at the same time, however, the transport energy used, as well as the ethical issues that come into play, when using imported products. There is always a strong environmental case for buying local products where possible.

NEW PATTERNS OF TRADE

Imaginative thinking about patterns of consumption and resource inefficiency is leading to new, safer economic models. A company in Chicago, for example, instead of selling you a washing machine, will loan you one, free of charge. It will service, repair or replace the machine when needed, simply charging you every time you wash your clothes. Instead of consumers buying, using and throwing out machines and then buying new ones, the company uses its expertise to reuse and recycle the same equipment for as long as each component will function. This model, which is also developing in the commercial carpet industry, rests on the same logic used by city-dwellers who are beginning to reject the car that stands idle for 22 out of 24 hours, instead hiring a car or using a taxi when they need one.

DOWNCYCLING

A new approach to recycling called downcycling is being developed alongside new, clean industrial processes. This involves salvaging discarded objects and material no longer

Recycled materials need not be
dull. This plastic material includes
bold, glowing colours (below).

suitable for use in their original form and reprocessing
them into the ingredients of new materials for other uses.
This is not something the householder can do, but we
should be aware that such products are beginning to come
onto the market. Examples include the shredding of paper
for reuse as insulating material or in lampshades, and the
grinding up of plastics to produce the material from which
plastic furniture, doormats and carpets can be made.
Attractive glass objects are made from recycled glass,
while some rubber flooring contains a high percentage of
used car tyres.

This new and radical re-orientation of industrial production and consumption has at its heart the traditional
wisdom of harbouring resources and designing with,
rather than against, nature. This offers designers and
home-makers exciting opportunities and the acceptance of
a much broader approach to style. In this way, environmental concerns, far from being limiting, provide the
springboard to create exciting and attractive homes that
display imagination and a unique, personal style.

HOME ENERGY SYSTEMS

New homes are now built to ever increasing standards of energy efficiency, but the options for improving existing homes are limited. While this book focuses largely on the contribution that elements of interior design and finishes can make towards sustainability, by far the greatest use of energy, in terms of natural resources and production of carbon emissions, comes from home heating and cooling systems. This chapter therefore explores the options available in this regard. It should be noted that the overarching aim must be to reduce carbon emissions and the use of non-renewable fuels, which as far as the homeowner is concerned means reducing energy consumption.

HOME ENERGY PERFORMANCE

An instructive first action is to measure your carbon footprint. Many web-based calculators make this an easy step-by-step process, and they are generally available on the web pages of the advisory organisations listed in the Sources section on page 198, such as the Energy Saving Trust. The more reliable calculators require you to enter either how much you spend on energy, or, for greater accuracy, the amount of energy in kWh (kilowatt hours) that your bills show you have used, with details about the size of your home, rather than just its generic type. Some calculators are sufficiently detailed to allow you to assess the impact of different hypothetical solutions such as double-glazing, changing boilers or other measures. Do be aware that this is an inexact science and it is worth consulting a number of websites, or for more accuracy call in an energy assessor, to be completely certain. Energy assessors can be located via the web.

Recent legislation in the UK means that every home that is sold will need to have an Energy Performance Certificate. Energy assessments have consequently become easy to obtain and you might usefully have one whether you are considering selling or not. These Certificates are similar to the certificates now given to domestic appliances by the Energy Saving Trust.

ENERGY PERFORMANCE CERTIFICATE

Charts recording a dwelling's performance aginst crucial aspects of environmental impact: energy use and amount of carbon dioxide produced.

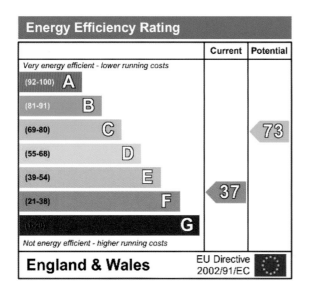

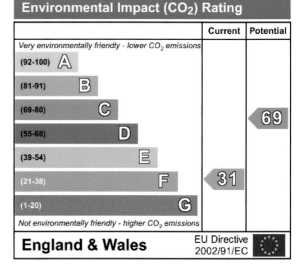

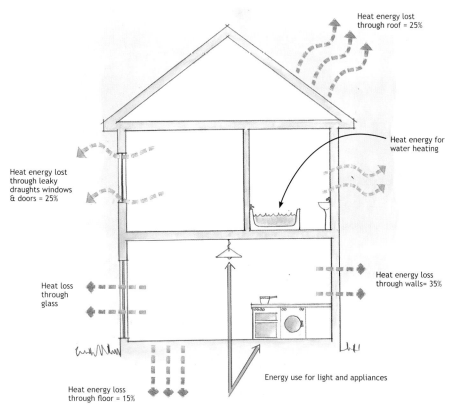

Heat energy lost through roof = 25%

Heat energy for water heating

Heat energy lost through leaky draughts windows & doors = 25%

Heat energy loss through walls= 35%

Heat loss through glass

Energy use for light and appliances

Heat energy loss through floor = 15%

Diagram illustrating the relative proportion of heat energy lost through different elements of a typical house.

According to the government's HIP (Home Information Pack) website:

A Certificate for a building gives the building an asset rating based on its energy efficiency, but doesn't take into account how the home is used by the occupiers. The Certificate will give the building a rating from A to G. An A rating shows it's very efficient, meaning lower fuel bills, while G is inefficient, meaning higher fuel bills. The Certificate will also show the building's environmental impact by indicating its carbon-dioxide emissions. There will also be recommendations for cost-effective actions to improve the building's rating. The potential rating is based on all the recommendations.

There are many variables to consider when planning actions to reduce your home's energy demand – efficiency in use, extent of maintenance, capital cost in relation to running costs, extent of embodied energy in equipment, no less than the extent of building work. The following broad strategies can be adopted to increase the sustainability of your home, and each will have a range of detailed options. They are listed in a broad order of benefit:

▶ Reducing your home's heating need – this is by far the most important action to take
▶ Increasing the efficiency of heating systems
▶ Reducing electricity consumption
▶ Heat recovery and healthy ventilation
▶ Generating your own electricity (micro-generation)
▶ Reducing water consumption

REDUCING HEAT DEMAND	COST	HEAT ENERGY SAVED
IMPROVING INSULATION	LOW/MED	HIGH
KEEPING HOME AT LOWER TEMPERATURE	REDUCED	MED/HIGH
INSULATING HOT WATER STORAGE TANKS	LOW	LOW/MED
IMPROVING DRAFT PROOFING/CONTROL VENTILATION	MED	MED/HIGH
IMPROVING EFFICIENCY OF HEAT INPUT		
INSTALLING CONDENSING GAS BOILER	MED	HIGH
HEATING USING GROUND SOURCE HEAT PUMPS	HIGH	VERY HIGH
INSTALLING SOLAR THERMAL WATER HEATING	MED	MED
REDUCING ELECTRICITY DEMAND	**COST**	**ELECTRICITY SAVED**
LOW-ENERGY LIGHT BULBS	LOW	HIGH
LOW-ENERGY A-RATED APPLIANCES	MINIMAL EXTRA	MED/HIGH
INSTALLING WIND TURBINE	VERY HIGH	MED/HIGH
INSTALLING PHOTOVOLTAIC SOLAR PANELS	VERY HIGH	MED/HIGH

Of the total energy consumed in the home, generally some 80 per cent is for space and water heating. This is a peak load in the order 15–35 kW depending upon the size of home, as compared with some 1.75–4 kW peak load for light and power for electrical appliances. This makes it clear that heating issues outweigh all others: achieving a small reduction in the energy you use for heat is much more worthwhile in environmental terms than a large reduction in electricity use for power and light. A reduction of 1°C in your home's temperature can save 10 per cent of heating costs. The equations are not straightforward, as the embodied energy of new equipment also needs to be considered, but generally reducing energy use is by far the most important strategy we should be pursuing in reducing the environmental impact of our homes. The above table gives an indication of what are broadly agreed to be effective measures relative to costs, but bear in mind they can only ever be roughly indicative given the extensive variety of dwellings and circumstances (for more information, see p.62).

Bear in mind that each of the sections are independent of each other – high electricity reduction is not comparable with high heat reduction.

A number of small, easy-to-install appliances are available which enable you to monitor your electricity consumption; others can reduce the consumption of fridges and freezers by optimising the power need of the appliance.

CENTRAL HEATING

Once you have reduced your overall heating demand (see pp.62–72 for a range of effective actions) the next step is to determine the most efficient heating technology that best suits your home.

While throwing away existing appliances to install new ones runs contrary to the important rule of sustainability, which requires things to be used for as long as possible, replacing inefficient heating or cooling appliances is an exception because new appliances are much more efficient than older ones and will immediately significantly reduce energy use and running cost. This does not necessarily mean replacing the whole heating installation – if pipe-work and radiators are in good condition then only the central heat-generating appliance (normally the boiler) need be replaced, just as when installing low energy light bulbs there is no need to replace the wiring system.

All space-heating systems consist of four generic components. While these components are in principle always the same, the detail design of each system will vary. The four components consist, in principle, of two that generate heat, and two that distribute it:

▶ Energy input in the form of fuel (e.g. gas, oil, biomass)
▶ An appliance that converts fuel energy into useable heat (e.g. a boiler)
▶ A system that distributes the heat to different spaces (pipe network)
▶ Heat emitters that warm the space by either radiated or convected heat (see pp. 68–71)

Heating systems that use electricity as their energy source (fuel) have in effect the same basic components, the difference being that the heat generating appliance is not in the home but at a central power station, with the energy distributed via the national grid. (This is termed 'central generation', as opposed to 'micro-generation' which refers to domestic generation of electricity – see p.183 for more details.)

HEAT GENERATION

Choosing the right heat-generating appliance can significantly reduce energy consumption, carbon emissions and running, so consider all the options before simply replacing an old system with a new version of the same type. Bear in mind that changing to a different system may involve disruption to floors, walls and decorations. When considering a new boiler ensure that the heat demand of your home is recalculated because not all old boilers were accurately sized to meet your home's heat demand and a new one may be smaller, thus saving money and energy use.

A key factor is the availability of fuel. Non-carbon-based fuels are increasingly available; these include plant-based fuels (biomass, biofuels), solar and wind power, and the heat energy that is stored in the ground. The most common heat-generating appliances are:

▶ High-efficiency boilers (usually gas but also oil and solid fuel)
▶ Biomass boilers
▶ Ground source heat pumps
▶ Combined heat and power

Solar thermal generators, used mainly for water heating, can also be used for general heating. All types of boilers must be serviced regularly to ensure that they operate at optimum efficiency.

HIGH EFFICIENCY BOILERS

Because they are efficient, easy to control and compact, and because of gas's widespread availability, gas boilers are the most common heat-generating appliance for central heating systems. All natural gas boilers now supplied in the UK are high-efficiency condensing boilers, which generally have an efficiency rating of 85–92 per cent, whereas older boilers, many of which still have many years of useful life, are only about 55–60 per cent efficient. Nevertheless, however efficient they may be, gas boilers still burn a finite natural resource and contribute to global warming.

Where town gas is not available boilers can perform exactly the same function if fuelled by bottled gas or oil. Modern versions are increasingly efficient, but they use oil-based products, as well as having the added environmental impact arising from the transport of the fuel. (Energy used for transport – embodied energy – is discussed on pp.34–6.)

STOVE

A high-efficiency 'clean-burn' wood-burning stove.

BIOMASS BOILERS

In principle biomass boilers can burn any growth crop that burns well, if in a form that can be easily fed into a boiler. Biofuel is sustainable because not only is it renewable, but the growth of the biofuel crop absorbs the same amount of carbon from the atmosphere as is emitted when burned. While trees are not, as yet, grown specially, new crops such as miscanthus and willow are being planted specifically as biofuels, an urgent debate is needed over the potential significant disruption to agricultural economies which arises from this switch to biofuel crops. Domestic biomass boilers function as part of central heating systems in the same way as gas boilers, and almost universally use either wood chips or wood pellets – the latter being the most efficient and economic.

The practicality and availability of biomass boilers for single dwellings is only now being tested in the UK, and the costs are still more than for gas or oil boilers, but prices are dropping as the technology and fuel supplies develop and the demand increases.

Other issues to deal with are the large areas required for fuel storage and the difficulty of delivery into urban sites. In order to minimise the expense and embodied energy of delivery, a large storage hopper is required. One that is 3.5 m long, 2 m wide and 1.5 m high will hold enough fuel for six months. This needs to be adjacent to the boiler so that the pellets can be fed automatically, and also near the lorry access. Underground hoppers are also possible but very expensive. Thus while biomass boilers in themselves have negligible environmental impact and are amongst the easiest to install inside existing homes, the full implications, including those of fuel delivery, mean that they may not be the most sustainable choice in all circumstances.

GROUND SOURCE HEAT PUMPS

Heat pumps can seem almost magical, as they appear to create something out of nothing, yet they are found in every home as the technology used in refrigerators. Used widely in Europe they are becoming increasingly available for heating. They work by exploiting the difference in temperature between one environment and another. The principle is that a refrigerant liquid in a sealed system, when expanded and contracted in cycles by an electric compressor pump, produces alternately heat and cold. This phenomenon means that the heat in the ground, which in winter remains at about 10–11°C, can be extracted, fed into a heat pump, which increases it to 30–40°C, which is high enough to be useful for heating. The process can be reversed in summer to provide cooling: heat is extracted from warm room air and 'dumped' into the ground or water. Water in a river or pond can be used instead of the ground.

Heat pumps are extraordinarily efficient in comparison with other heat generating appliances: for every 1 unit of energy input, an efficient gas boiler produces an output of 0.85–0.9 units of energy, while a heat pump produces 2.5–3 units of output. If the pump can be powered by solar- or wind-generated electricity (see below, pp.185–7) then a heat pump will create heat without consuming any resources and be carbon free.

Heat pumps are now widely available for small-scale domestic use, but they require a significant area of outside ground (or a pond) into which the absorption pipe can be laid. This is generally a continuous loop laid at a depth of no less than 75–90 cm. A rule of thumb is that 15 m of buried pipe is required for every kW generated. Where space is limited a pipe can be driven vertically deep into the ground, but this is an expensive operation.

Heat distribution is by means of a wet system – see below p.181. However, while most boilers produce water at 70–80°C, the 30–40°C produced by heat pumps means that a normal radiator system will not emit adequate heat, or will only give background warmth. To heat space to a comfortable 18–19°C will require larger than normal heat emitters – either much larger radiators or, more realistically, the large areas available with under floor heating. The benefits of under-floor heating are discussed on page 71.

If sufficient land is available and you can accommodate under-floor heating pipes, a heat pump is one of the most sustainable options for home heating, particularly as the equipment is simple and virtually maintenance free. At present installations are more

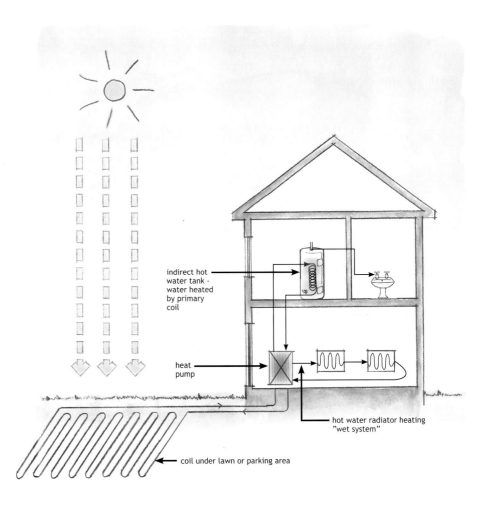

**GROUND SOURCE
HEAT PUMP**

Diagram showing the essential
components of a ground source
heat pump installation. A variant of
the absorbant coil could be placed
in a stream or pond.

indirect hot
water tank -
water heated
by primary
coil

heat
pump

hot water radiator heating
"wet system"

coil under lawn or parking area

expensive than traditional boiler-based systems but the cost is falling as demand grows.

Air source heat pumps are also available which avoid the need for buried coils – exactly as do fridges – but at present they have a very low efficiency and are expensive.

COMBINED HEAT AND POWER

Conventional electricity using gas or coal produces more heat than electricity (see below p.183) and systems exist to capture this heat; called Combined Heat and Power (CHP), they have for many years delivered heat to groups of homes in the vicinity of power stations. Standalone systems have long been available to generate electricity and to heat large buildings, but small CHP 'boilers' are now being developed for individual homes.

CHP boilers are about the size of a domestic fridge and generate approximately 1 kW of electricity and 2 kW of heat. Insufficient to heat the average home they offer a useful and free contribution to total heat demand. CHP boilers tend to be coupled with a gas boiler as a backup to cope with peak heating demand, and save in the order of 25 per cent of energy compared with separate installations of a gas boiler and mains electricity supply. One disadvantage is that in summer the unwanted heat is wasted.

While CHP systems are in principle efficient, simple to use and to install, with the advantage of being easily linked to a standard wet heat distribution system, the technology of small-scale domestic appliances has not proved as reliable as had been predicted, and they are not yet widely available.

or bar heaters. From an interior design point of view you need to consider a range of factors when considering heat emitters, such as their heat output in relation to the volume of the room, their position in relation to outside walls and windows, and limitations they impose on furnishing arrangements. Their appearance is also important and a wide range of designs is available, but all have to have a large enough surface area to emit the heat required by each space. Heat pumps generate lower temperature water so larger emitters are required, which will also be the case where children or older people are more than normally likely to touch the radiators: in this case low surface temperature radiators should be used.

The most common types of heat emitters are:
▶ Radiant panels: either piped water (wet systems) or electrical
▶ Radiators: actually only 30 per cent radiant and 70 per cent convecting depending upon pattern
▶ Underfloor heating: either wet or electrical
▶ Room stoves: wood or solid fuel, substantially radiant heat

Fan-assisted convector radiators on wet systems can save space, and are often installed under kitchen units where wall space is limited. An integral electric fan forces more air over a heating coil than in a normal radiator. These fans consume electricity, are expensive and should be avoided.

Heat can also be distributed from a central appliance by means of air ducted to each room. This used to be popular because of low installation cost, but air is a much less efficient method of heat transfer than water so air ducts have to be very much larger than water pipes; furthermore the fans which push the air through the ducts consume a large amount of electricity.

WATER HEATING

As heating water accounts for about 25 per cent of the energy consumption in the average home, any increase in

Like all home-generated electricity (as discussed in detail below, pp.183–7) you need to connect your electricity into the grid and will require your electricity supplier's agreement to do so.

HEAT DISTRIBUTION

By far the most common method of heat distribution around the home is a 'wet system': a network of pipes through which hot water is pumped to transmit the heat generated by a heat generator, such as a boiler, to the heat emitters: water-filled radiators or under-floor heating pipes. Water is a very efficient way of transferring heat, the instillations are simple and virtually maintenance free – apart from the circulating pump. All electric heating systems in principle use the same system without the water – a network of wires transmits the energy to panel the efficiency or reduction in heat input will be worthwhile. Water can be heated either by a standalone separate system or as part of a space heating installation, and in either case there are two types of systems – either direct or indirect. Direct systems heat cold water instantaneously as it passes through the heating appliance, while indirect systems heat water stored in a hot water storage tank, sometimes called a hot water cylinder. A key disadvantage of indirect water heating is that energy is used to heat stored water that may not be used for some time, while direct systems heat only the water required.

BOILER TYPES FOR HOT WATER

Most gas central heating boilers come with the option of providing direct or indirect water heating, as do the other heat generating appliances discussed above. In small homes where a small amount of water is used at any one time, direct water heating is both efficient and practical. Space heating boilers that do this are sometimes called 'combi' boilers. However, in a larger home where a number of bathrooms may be used at the same peak periods an indirect system will ensure an adequate supply to all taps. A balance between storing hot water that is used only occasionally needs to be considered, so if two or three bathrooms are used intermittently, for example occasional guest bathrooms, it is more energy efficient for each bathroom to have its own local direct water heating.

Most new hot-water cylinders are pre-insulated; significant savings can be made on older tanks by wrapping them with a proper insulation jacket.

SOLAR THERMAL COLLECTIONS

Solar thermal energy (as distinct from solar electrical energy discussed below on pp.186–7) can be used both to heat water and to a small degree to warm space (see pp.66–7).

Collecting solar energy to heat water is an established technology, and although there are many variations in detail, all systems work essentially on the same simple principles: the sun is collected by a heat absorbing surface which heats water as it flows or is pumped through a heat collector, and this hot water heats a coil inside an insulated storage tank, where it heats the water.

A temperature of about 60°C is generally required for domestic hot water and temperature in excess of this can be achieved with solar water heating outside the summer months of peak sunshine. But in periods of substantial cloud cover an alternative heat source is needed. Even in periods of low sunshine solar collectors generate a degree of pre-heating so that the energy required by the alternative source to heat the water is reduced. As a rule of thumb, solar water heating systems in the UK can reduce energy demand for water heating by 50 per cent. If the supplementary heat input in winter, and the power for the circulating pump, can be from another renewable source then your hot water will be entirely sustainable.

Solar water systems require little maintenance apart from the pump; whether you can dispense with a pump and rely on gravity circulation will depend on the configuration of your home, and whether you have supplementary booster heating.

It is simple to add a solar water heating system to an existing home, and different types are available for different circumstances. Systems can either stand alone or be linked into existing indirect hot water systems. However linked systems require a storage tank with two heater coils, one for the solar heating and one for the 'main' system from the boiler. It is not possible to link solar systems to direct 'combi' space heating systems.

Solar panels can be mounted on either flat or pitched roofs providing that these are not overshadowed, and the more directly south facing the more efficient, but adequate solar heat is still available if panels face south-west or south-east. As demand grows and with increasingly efficient equipment the cost of solar thermal installations will fall: at the time of writing it is generally considered that they pay for themselves in 7–9 years, and this will come down as energy costs increase. After that time, and given the non-existent maintenance costs, your hot water will be free.

In latitudes with significant sunshine even when the air temperature is cold and homes still need heat, solar thermal energy may provide a surplus of hot water, and this can supplement space heating. There are a range of such hybrid systems, which although not comprehensive heating systems, will make a useful carbon-free contribution to total space heating.

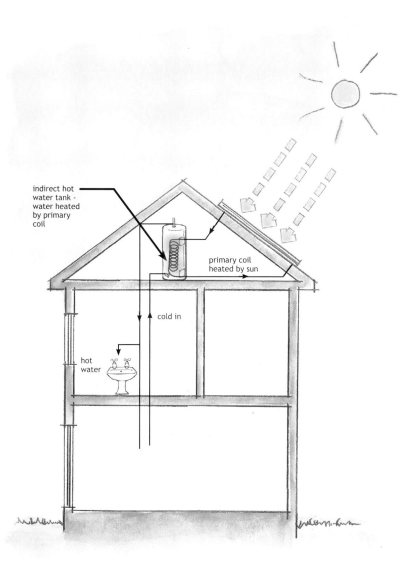

Diagram showing the essential principles of a roof-mounted solar (thermal) water heater.

indirect hot water tank - water heated by primary coil

primary coil heated by sun

cold in

hot water

ELECTRICITY GENERATION

Once it has been generated electricity is an efficient, clean and simple energy source requiring little maintenance, which is why it is so universally valued. However, traditional electricity generating power stations use vast quantities of non-renewable natural gas or coal, emit a significant proportion of all greenhouse gasses to the atmosphere, and are extremely inefficient. In most power stations a massive 70 per cent of the energy input goes to waste mainly in the form of heat, and in so-called efficient power stations still only 45 per cent of the energy input is turned into electricity. Hence the urgent need for alternative methods of electricity generation, and for households to reduce their electricity consumption.

Large-scale wind farms in Northern Europe and solar farms in hotter climates such as Spain and California demonstrate what can be achieved by centralised renewable generation, and renewable generation is growing, albeit slowly, in the UK. Most UK central suppliers source a small proportion of their electricity from renewable fuels, but this is still only 2 per cent of total electricity. Government policy is not encouraging the growth of renewable technologies in any very

WIND POWER
A typical horizontal-axis wind
generator.

productive manner, and a huge policy bias remains towards traditional non-renewable fuels, which means that the true cost of our electricity is hidden. One of the few wholly 'green' generating companies, 'Ecotricity', is increasing renewable capacity by investing all its profits into the construction of wind farms, as one of a few small truly renewable generators that are entering the market.

Switching your supplier so that you buy electricity from a renewable supplier is a very simple and constructive step towards making your home more sustainable, and will have only a marginal additional cost. This is an important step that everyone should take. An alternative strategy is to generate your own – this is known as micro-generation.

The technologies of micro-generation using sun or wind are advancing rapidly, becoming more user friendly with prices falling as demand increases. Nevertheless they are not yet economic; the table on p.176 shows that at present there are still other, more economic, options for reducing energy use.

One of the major stumbling blocks with renewable micro-generation is the mismatch between the occasions when sun or wind are available, and the periods when power is required, which means that a method of storing electricity is necessary: at present the only option is in a costly array of batteries.

Consequently, as most dwellings are connected to the national supply grid, the current available alternative is to use the national grid as, in effect, a 'storage pool': when you generate electricity you feed it into the national grid, for which you receive a credit, and then draw electricity from the grid as and when you need it. The grid effectively acts as a huge national pool of electricity into and from which micro-generators can feed and draw electricity as needed. For those homes not on the grid the principles of micro-generation outlined below are the same, except that they must have battery storage facilities.

In the UK the peak electricity consumption for light and power (i.e. excluding heating) in the average home is in the range of 1.75–4.0 kW. Yet the amount of peak power that it is currently practical to produce with domestic sized wind or solar installations is a capacity in the order of 0.75–1.5 kW, depending upon available space, local conditions, orientation, etc. Meeting the full peak domestic electrical demand even for light and power requires larger installations than are currently practical. And with current costs of equipment, and given the low price paid to homeowners for any electricity they feed to the grid, the cost of micro-generation is unlikely to be recovered in less than about twenty years and probably more. Furthermore, although difficult to be definitive in the infancy of these new technologies, today's micro-generating equipment is likely to need replacing in about the same number of years. Consequently micro-generation is not yet a sensible first priority for reducing the environmental impact of the home, but could become so if, in the UK, government ensured that prices were tilted in favour of micro-generation.

This is not to say that small installations of the more economic size of 0.75–1.0 kW capacity are not useful – they can make an important contribution as part of a whole house efficiency drive which would include reducing demand, increasing insulation levels, maximising passive solar energy, and the other measures discussed in this book, because every ounce of CO_2 saved is worth saving.

WIND POWER

Even in relatively windless areas there is often sufficient wind to generate some electricity. Factors that need to be taken into account in assessing the viability of a wind system are local wind speed, the effect of adjacent properties on the flow of wind, and the size and height of generator that are practical. However the comments above about what it is currently practical to achieve at a domestic scale apply; capacity is unlikely to meet total peak domestic demand, except in rural areas where large wind generators are a realistic possibility.

There are two types of wind generator: the more traditional horizontal wind turbines, of which there are many on the market, and vertical-axis turbines. The latter are seldom seen in the UK but in the US, Canada and Europe they are proving effective for small-scale

Figures for the relative costs per tonne of carbon dioxide saved over a lifetime using different energy systems are difficult to quantify accurately because there are so many variables, however a rough order of costs for an average three-bedroom semi-detached home gives a useful guide as to what is sensible:

Biomass pellet boiler	£50–£110
Ground source heat pumps	£65–£120
Solar hot water	£460 - £600
Photovoltaic electricity (assuming 50 per cent of electricity is exported to grid)	£355–£645
Wind generated electricity	no statistics are yet available but likely to be less than photovoltaic electricity.

installations. Vertical-axis turbines have many advantages over the horizontal type: as they suffer fewer internal stresses they are relatively maintenance free, they induce fewer structural stresses on buildings or masts on which they are mounted. Most importantly they can accommodate wind turbulence induced by surrounding buildings, and they are virtually silent in operation. It is therefore likely that vertical-axis turbines will increasingly become available in the UK.

Apart from the wind turbine and its mounting the other components required for a wind system are a rectifier, which smoothes out the power as wind speed fluctuates, and an inverter, to convert the direct current (DC), suitable for batteries, into alternating current (AC), for compatibility with the grid and normal appliances. Neither is particularly large and would normally be mounted adjacent to the mains electrical incoming supply and fuse boards.

When considering the use of a wind turbine, specialist analysis of conditions at your site is necessary, and must include a survey of wind speeds over a period of time, and assessment of any wind 'shadows' and turbulence caused by surrounding buildings and trees. Consideration of the likely visual impact on neighbours is essential as well as consultation with the local planning authority to establish if planning consent is required. While planning restrictions are generally being eased different authorities have different attitudes - some now allow small installations without the need for planning consent. It is also essential to ascertain that your local mains electricity supplier will accept your electricity into the grid.

SOLAR POWER (PHOTOVOLTAICS)

Electricity is generated by the action of both light and heat energy on chemically coated glass, or plastics, called photovoltaic cells or panels. There is a range of different types, the finer technical details of which don't concern a general outline such as this. The efficiency of conversion of solar energy into electricity is in the range of 5–20 per cent, which when combined with the complexity and high cost of manufacture means that at present photovoltaic technology is expensive in comparison with wind power. But the technology is developing rapidly and with increases in demand costs are likely to fall. The life expectancy of current generation photovoltaic panels is considered to be about 20 years – similar to that of wind generators.

Cost aside, photovoltaic panels are a practical and easy to use technology and can easily be added to existing buildings regardless of location, provided they are not overshadowed by taller buildings or trees. They are noiseless, and apart from occasional cleaning are maintenance free. Solar panels on roofs are now generally accepted by planning and regulatory bodies except on historic buildings. Most types are formed into panels or sheets for fixing either on top of existing roof coverings or integrated into tiles or slates. Glass based PV panels can also make attractive canopies on structures such as walkways, pergolas, cycle sheds, or can be freestanding panels on the ground or flat roofs, or even as facings to walls. Their orientation and angle of inclination need to be carefully calculated for maximum efficiency in each particular location – installations generally require

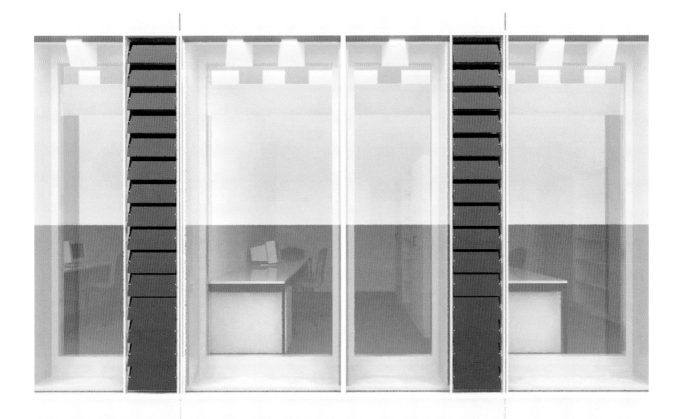

VENTILATION

The design of external walls is developing so that they respond to environmental conditions – in this case variable louvers provide natural ventilation.

specialist design although on-line guidance is available – see www.energysavingtrust.org.uk.

As for wind power the electricity generated needs to be converted to AC current for feeding into the grid and you need to ensure that your supplier will accept the electricity generated.

VENTILATION

As discussed in chapter 2 good ventilation is essential to the healthy home, and plays an important part in a home's energy efficiency. In most older homes draughts and uncontrolled opening of windows for fresh air is estimated to waste between 15 and 22 per cent of heat – hence the importance of 'sealing tight, ventilating right'. Whole house ventilation systems not only save energy but control humidity, remove polluted air and generally create a healthier and more comfortable internal environment. They have been widespread in Continental Europe for some time.

Stale air is extracted from and fresh air introduced into the dwelling through ducts connected to a small fan, usually located in the loft. This sends stale air to the outside, while bringing fresh air in through the roof. The fan runs continuously and has a very low power rating, using some 40–75 watts – the size of a small traditional light bulb – depending upon fan speed settings. Small installations extract air only from kitchens and bathrooms, drawing air into these rooms naturally from other rooms via doorways, while more comprehensive systems have air ducted to and from all rooms. In older properties, where the installation takes up space and you want to minimise disruption it is worth observing which rooms suffer the worst condensation in order to decide

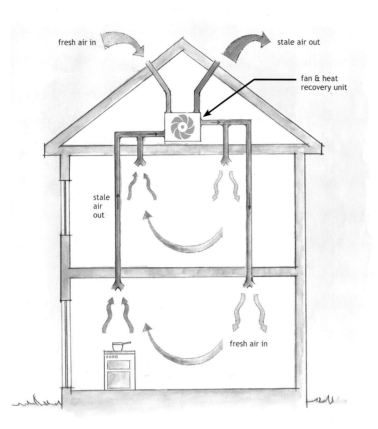

fresh air in

stale air out

fan & heat
recovery unit

stale
air
out

fresh air in

Diagram illustrating the principles of a whole house ventilation system, showing the stale but warm air passing through a heat exchanger/fan unit which extracts the heat which is used to warm cold incoming fresh air.

which should be served in addition to kitchens and bathrooms. In all but hot climates the fans are fitted with heat exchangers that extract the heat from the stale air, and use this to warm the fresh incoming air from outside which may be cold. They generally recover between 70–95 per cent of the existing heat – thus reducing much of the heat lost through ventilation.

Whole house ventilation systems are in principle simple to install and require only a 13-amp power supply. In single story dwellings with lofts, and on the upper level of houses the disruption is minimal as the ducts run in the loft and require only ceiling grills. The main difficulty, which can be significant in older properties, comes when routing ducts through upper floors down to the ceiling outlets in lower floors. Most rooms will require ducts which can be plastic or metal of 100 mm diameter or rectangular size 250 x 60 mm, or for large rooms and kitchens 150 mm diameter or rectangular 250 x 75 mm.

Accommodating ducts without disrupting furniture layouts can be difficult in existing buildings – they are ideally routed to ground floor rooms through built-in bedroom wardrobes, storage or circulation spaces on upper floors.

Commonly smaller systems are controlled simply with an on/off switch or with a humidity sensor for automatic use, but in larger systems controllers can vary the rates of air change in different parts of the house. The fan and technology systems are simple and well established, the only maintenance being the fan component, which can have dust and pollen filter units. These filters are useful for hay-fever sufferers, but these systems should not be considered as providing full air conditioning. Systems are not very expensive and while they need to be sized and designed by a specialist, the technology is simple enough to be fitted by most builders, who are becoming increasingly familiar with them.

WATER CONSUMPTION

Where we are fortunate enough to have a supply of water, the key issue affecting the environment is not so much the use of water per se, but the high energy use involved in supplying high-quality drinking water – in collecting, treating, storing and distributing it. The drive towards sustainability therefore should focus on a reduction in the use of treated water, not only by reducing the total amount of drinking quality water used, but also by switching to untreated rainwater wherever possible. The issue becomes clear when considering garden watering or car washing for which there is absolutely no good reason to use expensively treated drinking-quality water, when rainwater is perfectly adequate and free.

By installing low-flow appliances – i.e spray taps, low flush WCs and 'A-rated' washing machines – water consumption can be reduced by 25 per cent. Flushing WCs uses 25 per cent of household water, so if not replacing your cistern you can install one of a number of water reducing devices such as a 'Water Hippos' or 'Save-a-Flush'. Another 25 per cent can be saved by careful management and reduction of use – such as not leaving taps running and using bowls for rinsing dishes and clothes: a 50 per cent reduction in your household water consumption is significant: it will save money and be a very positive environmental contribution.

The first and easiest step in reducing the amount of treated water used is to collect rainwater from roofs into barrels or 'butts' for outdoor use. Simple rainwater harvesting kits can be cheaply installed on down-pipes. Going a step further there are systems that connect into your plumbing so that rainwater is collected, stored, filtered and pumped for use to flush WCs and in washing machines. These systems have an automatic mains water valve to ensure the tank is topped-up if the amount of stored rainwater falls below a minimum level. Most such systems have underground storage tanks. Although these more comprehensive systems require significant plumbing works, this will not necessarily be too disruptive if undertaking new bathroom or utility room installations, and with the increasing cost of water they are certainly worth considering.

WATER BUTT

A simple water harvesting system connected to a down-pipe, for use in watering the garden or washing the car.

ELECTRICAL APPLIANCES

ENERGY SAVING TRUST LABEL

This label is applied to appliances recommended by the Energy Saving Trust.

Energy

Washing machine

Manufacturer
Model

More efficient

A
B
C
D
E
F
G

B

Less efficient

Energy consumption kWh/cycle
(based on standard test results for 60°C cotton cycle)   1.05

Actual energy consumption will depend on how the appliance is used.

Washing performance
A: higher G: lower   **A** B C D E F G

Spin drying performance
A: higher G: lower   A **B** C D E F G

Spin speed (rpm)   1400

Capacity (cotton) kg   5.0
Water consumption *l*   55

THE EUROPEAN ENERGY LABEL

The European Energy label indicates the energy efficiency of an appliance. It includes water consumption where appropriate and a voluntary indication of noise levels.

USING ENERGY-EFFICIENT APPLIANCES can significantly reduce your home's consumption of electricity. A household equipped with all the most efficient appliances available would consume only one-third of the electricity used by one with the most inefficient appliances. Choosing energy-efficient models is particularly important with appliances that are permanently switched on, such as refrigerators and freezers. In the UK these appliances alone consume almost as much electricity as all the office buildings combined. Televisions and videos on stand-by mode are also permanently 'on' and waste energy. If all the televisions in the US were left on standby, they would use as much power as the Chernobyl nuclear power station.

Selecting energy-efficient appliances is good for your pocket as well as good for the earth. They may be more expensive to buy initially, but this will be offset by savings in fuel – particularly if fuel costs rise. Although good practice normally encourages the long-term use of goods, this does not apply to old electrical appliances. The latest efficient appliances consume so much less energy that it is sounder to discard old inefficient models and buy new ones. Furthermore, governments and electricity suppliers sometimes subsidize the cost of energy-efficient machines as part of their commitment to energy saving. When buying the top-rated appliances you get a much better model than you are paying for. Guidance for purchasers exists in the form of energy-efficiency labels that rate products from A to G. In the UK, look for European Energy and Energy Saving Trust labels, and in the USA, the Energy Star certification and Energy Guide programmes.

Appliances have other environmental impacts: for example, water and detergent use in washers, are also assessed on the label. The noise level of an appliance may also appear on the label but this is voluntary in the UK. For other aspects, consult the manufacturer's literature. When buying and using electric appliances, use the following points as a guide:

GENERAL GUIDELINES

▶ When choosing appliances, be guided by the amount of energy consumed in use rather than in production, since this will have the greater environmental impact. Look for energy-efficiency labels.

▶ Choose gas appliances whenever possible. They use less energy, are cheaper to run than electrical models and produce fewer emissions. Have them checked regularly to make sure they are burning properly to avoid carbon monoxide poisoning.

▶ Keep all appliances well maintained to increase their

efficiency: defrost refrigerators and freezers, clean the refrigerant coils behind refrigerators, unblock filters in washers and vents in driers.

▶ Don't rely on energy saving plugs. They appear to work only on older appliances

▶ Choose the smallest appliance that suits your needs.

▶ Run appliances on night-tariff electricity, but beware of any noise that might disturb neighbours. Night-tariff electricity is not only cheaper but also uses power that is more efficiently generated than peak-time electricity.

▶ Dispose of equipment to proper recycling stations. Take refrigerators to certified locations because of the dangerous refrigerant gases.

COOKING APPLIANCES

▶ If you do use an electric cooker, choose the most efficient cooking elements. Best are induction hobs, followed by ceramic hobs and ring elements. Solid disc hotplates are the least efficient.

▶ Use a jug-style kettle to boil only the amount of water needed. But boiling water on a gas cooker uses less energy than using electric kettles.

FRIDGES AND FREEZERS

▶ Select AA rated items

▶ Select a refrigerator that has natural gas rather than HFC refrigerants.

▶ Make sure that there is adequate ventilation around fridges and freezers. A poorly ventilated refrigerator can use as much as 90 per cent more energy.

▶ Don't place a refrigerator or freezer next to a cooker or other hot appliances. It will have to work harder and consume more energy.

▶ Set your refrigerator and freezer to the highest temperature at which they will work efficiently. Some models have special eco-settings

▶ Special features are expensive to run: icemaking consumes up to 25 per cent and auto-defrost up to 40 per cent additional electricity.

▶ Use a cool larder if you have one to store as many foods as possible and have a smaller refrigerator. Larder storage is also better for some foods.

WASHING MACHINES AND DISHWASHERS

▶ Buy a washing machine with a horizontal axis clothes drum rather than a tub type. They use less energy, less water and are gentler on clothes.

▶ Wash clothes and dishes at lowest possible temperatures – 40°C rather than 60°C is adequate, except for oil and grease soiling.

▶ Always run machines on full loads.

▶ Locate hot fill washing machines and dishwashers as close to the hot water source as possible

▶ Dry clothes on a line whenever possible.

▶ Choose a ventilating clothes drier – more efficient than a condensing drier.

TELEVISIONS, AUDIO EQUIPMENT AND COMPUTERS

▶ Never leave a television, video or stereo in standby mode. It remains permanently on and the total electricity used can amount to 80 per cent of that used when the machine is actually in use.

▶ If you have equipment with transformers, switch the transformer as well as the appliance off when not in use.

▶ When replacing small appliances such as battery chargers, external path lights, burglar alarms and doorbells, choose solar-powered versions. None will make a great difference to the total energy consumption of your home but every little helps.

▶ Keep your computer equipment, particularly the monitor, switched off when not in use. If it is essential to keep equipment on standby, the 'sleep' or 'energy-save' mode takes only 10 per cent of the energy consumed by leaving it fully on.

▶ Construction of computers is highly energy intensive. If possible, choose a manufacturer who recycles computer parts.

ECO-LABELLING

INCREASING UNDERSTANDING OF THE IMPORTANCE OF ENVIRONMENTAL ISSUES has prompted a raft of products on the market that are supposedly environmentally sound. Many manufacturers use meaningless terms such as 'environmentally friendly' or 'kind to nature' without substantiating these claims. But consumer concern has also given rise to independent organizations that assess and certify whether products are truly ecologically sound and sustainable. Although a universal standard is impossible for all products everywhere, eco-labels identify the extent to which a product is designed and manufactured to have the minimum environmental impact. Some eco-label schemes are government funded. Others charge manufacturers for assessing their products and this sometimes means that equally safe products from smaller companies may be excluded for reasons of expense.

The criteria used in labelling schemes vary from organization to organization but all broadly consider most of the issues covered in this book:

▶ Resource depletion

▶ Energy demand

▶ Avoidance of chemicals in manufacture

▶ Avoidance of chemical emissions

▶ Avoidance of chemical residues and offgassing

▶ Biodegradability

▶ Ethical issues.

The 22-member Global Eco-labelling Network attempts to co-ordinate standards worldwide and publicizes all assessments from their member organizations. These are available on the Internet: www.gen.gr.jp.

Ethical and fair trade issues are usually covered by separate certifying organizations. The Rugmark, for example, ensures that rugs are ethically made without enforced or child labour and that companies pay proper wages and sponser children's educational programmes. Claims by retailers and suppliers that their products are safe and ethically produced although uncertified should be viewed with some scepticism, since there is little that the consumer can do to verify such claims. Energy labelling schemes measure only the energy efficiency of an appliance in use and, where appropriate, its water consumption. In Europe look for Energy Labels and in the USA, Energy Star labels (see p.192).

From the point of view of the homemaker, looking for eco-labels is probably the most realistic way to shop safely. Failing that, we can only subject each product to our own assessment according to the issues outlined in the book. Manufacturers are increasingly posting detailed specifications of their products on the Internet and this is now a valuable source of information.

The following lists a selection of reliable labelling organizations. For their websites, see p. 186.

BLUE ANGEL (GERMANY)
One of the oldest and most comprehensive labelling systems. Certifies more than 3,000 products including many items for the home.

ECO-LABELLING (EUROPEAN UNION)
Certifies appliances, personal computers, textiles and some furnishings, including mattresses.

ENVIRONMENTAL CHOICE (CANADA)

Certifies a wide range of domestic products, including appliances, paints, adhesives, carpets and building materials.

GREEN SEAL (USA)

Sponsored by the United States Environmental Protection Agency. Certifies a few houshold products including paint, windows and cleaning materials.

OKO TEX 100

Certifies eastern European and Asian fabrics

SOIL ASSOCIATION

Certifies food, textiles, timber and garden products that have been produced and processed to strict organic, chemical-free controls and standards.

GUT (GERMANY)

Label of a group of European manufacturers producing carpet that is environmentally safe in all aspects from raw materials to laying. Has an excellent, multilingual website.

FORESTRY STEWARDSHIP COUNCIL

Worldwide certification programme for wood and wood-derived products including engineered boards and wallpaper.

NORDIC SWAN (SCANDINAVIA)

Certifies many consumer products including appliances, home furnishings and building materials.

USA CARPET INDUSTRY 'GREEN LABEL' PROGRAMME

Voluntary code for carpets with low chemical content. Some UK manufacturers also adhere to this standard.

CHEMICALS

No list can identify every dangerous chemical. Nor is it the case that the presence of the chemicals listed will automatically make you ill – the extent to which they affect individuals depends on the age, general health and living environment of the person concerned. All that I aim to do here is to increase awareness and identify the worst and most commonly found dangers. Listed below are common chemicals in paints, adhesives and many plastics that should be avoided. Many have a number of different names, some of which are given in brackets. These chemicals are identified in a number of registers, including the US Environmental Protection Agency's Green Seal testing program (see p.195), as known or possible carcinogens or environmental pollutants.

Chemicals are used not only for primary functions, such as to provide colour or adhesion, but also for less obvious purposes such as binding, dispersing, filling, softening, hardening and plasticizing, and as antifoaming, and bactericidal agents. Yet more chemicals are needed to ensure that all these ingredients combine and work together. By contrast, organic products contain only naturally occurring ingredients that are generally compatible with our biological systems.

It is impossible to list the health consequences of all chemicals. These range from mild effects such as headaches and respiratory irritations, to more serious conditions such as asthma, reproductive problems and cancers. Chemicals can also have behavioural and performance consequences ranging from mild to severe cases of fatigue, irritability, memory impairment, inability to concentrate and mood disorders. Environmental effects include polluting emissions to air, land and water, photochemical smog and ozone depletion.

When choosing products for the home, take time to consider the safety of the ingredients as well as visual and practical aspects. Use materials that are as close as possible to their natural state and have the fewest chemical ingredients, unless there is an overriding reason not to do so. Be particularly careful to check the ingredients of materials used in kitchens, bedrooms and children's rooms, particularly if preparing a room for a new baby. Also take extra care when choosing materials that are likely to be abraded or get hot or wet – such conditions will make them more likely to release their toxic ingredients. Remember when fixing materials to make sure that adhesives are also safe. Choose those that do not contain borax, formaldehyde, halogenated solvents, heavy metals, or more more than 5 per cent of VOC solvents.

There are millions of chemicals in use today. This list does not claim to be exhaustive, nor does the omission of any chemical in any way imply it is safe. Comprehensive chemical references are cited in the sources list (p.182) and bibliography (p.191).

▶ 1,2–Dichlorobenzene
▶ 1,1,1–Trichlorethane (TCE)
▶ Acetic aldehydes
▶ Acrolien (Acrylaldehyde, Propenol, Ethylene aldehyde)
▶ Acrylonitrile (Vinyl cyanide VCN)
▶ Antimony.
▶ Benzene and Benzyl chlorides
▶ Cadmium
▶ Chlorofluorocarbons (CFCs)
▶ Chlorotoluene
▶ Dichlorobenzines
▶ Ethanol
▶ Ethanol glycol and Ethelyne oxide
▶ Ethylbenzine (EB)
▶ Formaldehyde (Methal aldehyde, Methal oxides, Formalin)
▶ Halogenated hydrocarbons
▶ Lead
▶ Mercury
▶ Methanol
▶ Methyl ethyl ketone (MEK)
▶ Methyl napthalene
▶ Methyline chloride (dichloromethane)
▶ Naptha
▶ Napthalene
▶ N-butyl alcohol
▶ Polyisociantes,
▶ Propylene
▶ Propylene glycol and oxide (Epoxy propane)
▶ Polyurethanes
▶ Pthalates (DEHP, BEHP and DOP)
▶ Toluene
▶ Styrenes (Phenylethelene, Vinyl benzine)
▶ Vinyl chloride (VCM)
▶ White spirit (aliphatic hydrocarbons)
▶ Xylene

CHECKLIST

THIS CHECKLIST SUMMARIZES THE ACTIONS you can take that do not require major building work or disruptions in your home. Greater environmental efficiency will require more extensive changes – see pp.172–89.

APPLIANCES AND LIGHTS

▶ Buy energy-efficient appliances (see p.192–3).
▶ Use dishwashers and washing machines only at full capacity.
▶ Don't keep a refrigerator running for only a few items.
▶ Select long-lasting equipment and equipment designed for disassembly.
▶ Service all equipment, particularly microwaves, regularly.
▶ Use low-energy lightbulbs.
▶ Use sensors or time clocks so that hallway or outdoor lights are not left on when not needed.
▶ Never use the standby option on televisions and audio equipment.
▶ Use solar-powered versions of small appliances such as battery chargers, doorbells and alarms.
▶ Unplug appliances such as electric blankets before getting into bed.
▶ Keep one metre away from electrical appliances if possible.
▶ Have all gas appliances serviced and tested for carbon monoxide emissions regularly.

HEATING AND ENERGY CONSUMPTION

▶ Reduce the peak temperature in your home.
▶ Reduce the temperature of hot water for bathing (maximum 55°C) and for washing clothes and dishes (maximum 40°C).
▶ Fit thermostats/programmable controls on appliances and follow patterns of use rather than keeping water and rooms heated when not needed.
▶ Reduce the amount of hot water you store. Combine water heating with space heating boilers.
▶ Lag hot water tanks and pipes.
▶ Locate heat emitters for maximum efficiency and put reflectors behind radiators on outside walls.
▶ Use radiant panel heaters wherever possible.
▶ Draughtproof your home and increase insulation, particularly of lofts, but make sure there is adequate ventilation.
▶ Install passive ventilation devices (see p.76) instead of electric fans.
▶ Maximize solar gain (see p.66).
▶ Buy electricity from suppliers who generate power from renewable sources.

MATERIALS AND FURNISHINGS

▶ Use as few applied finishes as possible particularly avoiding non-organic paints (see p.132).
▶ Select sturdy items of furniture that will last a long time.
▶ Use recycled items.
▶ Repair and extend the useful life of as many things as possible.
▶ Use local materials and suppliers.
▶ Choose naturally occurring, organic, biodegradable materials.
▶ If you do need chemically-based products, try to avoid the chemicals listed on p.196.
▶ Choose products made in closed-loop processes (see pp.30–31).
▶ Buy from ethical producers whenever possible.
▶ Avoid using materials in short supply or from protected resources.
▶ If possible, choose products that are certified by a reputable eco-labelling organization (see p.194–5).

REDUCING WASTE AND SAVING WATER

▶ Buy as few packaged goods as possible.
▶ Recycle as much solid waste as you can: paper, cardboard, aluminium, steel, glass, plastics.
▶ Compost all biodegradable kitchen waste.
▶ Take used appliances and furniture to repair and reuse organisations.
▶ Take small household objects and clothes to secondhand shops.
▶ Take showers rather than baths.
▶ Don't install water-hungry power showers.
▶ Put a brick in your WC cistern to save water used in flushing.
▶ Collect rainwater in butts for watering the garden.

SOURCES

Since the first edition of this book the availability and awareness of sustainable building methods, materials and energy issues has grown significantly, and the web now offers access to almost universal information – whether advisory information and guidance, the availability of materials and from where they may be purchased. As a key aim of the book is to aid the implementation of sustainable actions in the home this new list of sources identifies the web pages for advisory organisations – both governmental and not for profit – that offer guidance and information on sustainable issues affecting the home, as well as trade associations with lists of members. Many companies offer a range of renewable energy systems and can be found on the web. Many are accredited with web links. A few are cited below because their web sites include helpful information and guidance. Their inclusion in no way suggests an endorsement of the company, its products or service, nor does the exclusion of any company imply views about that company. One key point to remember: whatever you may be buying choose locally produced and supplied goods wherever possible.

ADVISORY SITES AND INFORMATION PORTALS

AECB (Association fro Environment-Conscious Building)
www.aecb.net
Mainly for members in the construction industry, but considerable amounts of information accessible to non-members, including a directory of suppliers and construction professionals, with links to their websites.

Beyond Oil
www.fraw.org.uk
Idiosyncratic campaigning website with downloads on wide range of policy issues; useful analysis of government policies and media hype aimed at reduction as the only viable strategy; excellent bibliography including practical guidance.

Centre for Alternative Technology (CAT)
www.cat.org
Groundbreaking work on every aspect of sustainability; comprehensive reference and advisory information in clear, jargon free fact-sheets; online shop with extensive range of books; some building and micro generation products. Consultancy service. Excellent place to start any search.

Energy Saving Trust
www.est.org.uk
Substantial research and information resource, aiming to reduce carbon emissions and encourage action by businesses and homeowners offering comprehensive advice, including grant availability. Accreditation and eco-labelling system, tests and recommends energy efficient domestic appliances. Local network of advisory service. Essential reading.

Environnent Agency
www.environment-agency.gov.uk
Concerned with water use and flooding issues. Advice on water-saving strategies.

Environmental Choice (Canada)
www.ecologo.org
Publishes extensive screening of large range of household products; useful resume of the potential hazards of generic household and decorating products, and lists those that avoid them. Some products may not be available in UK.

Environmental Protection UK
www.environmental-protection.org.uk
Advisory network offering downloadable information on controlling environmental pollution, including air quality and noise.

Ethical Consumer Research Association

www.ethicalconumer.org
'(ECRA) is a not-for-profit organisation . . . to promote universal human rights, environmental sustainability and animal welfare . . . researching and publishing information on companies and their products.' Website with reports on ethical standards and magazine available by subscription.

Ethical Junction

www.ethicaljnunction.org
'A portal for all things ethical . . . to provide a universal ethical resource to the public. . . . an independent not-for-profit Community Interest Company, the web site includes EthicalSearch® our screened ethical search engine, directory listings, an ethical advertising network.'

European eco-label catalogue

www.eco-label.com
Certification of wide range of products, claims to certify only safe products with the lowest environmental impact providing they perform as well as alternative products. Identifies availability by country

Forestery Stewardship Council (FSC)

www.fsc-uk.org
Identifies properly managed timber and excludes protected species; lists criteria and controls and methods, useful lists of suppliers and also joinery manufacturers.

Freecycle

http://uk.freecycle.org/
National network facilitating free exchange and recycling. 'Our gaol is to keep useable items out of landfill . . . manufacture fewer goods and lessen the impact on the earth.'

Green Choices

www.greenchoices.org
Suppliers of sustainable materials and products.

Green Consumer Guide

www.greenconsumerguide.com
Independent portal for information on wide range of issues including domestic energy, building, cleaning, electrical goods, food, etc.

Green Specification

www.greenspec.co.uk
Comprehensive technical information and specifications for the professional on every aspect of building sustainability, clear source for range of suppliers.

National Energy Foundation

www.nef.org
'Promoting a better use of energy to counter climate change.' A good place to start: wide ranging advice: brief reviews of renewable technologies, links to other sites, info on grants and a 'jargon buster', carbon calculator, consultancy service.

Oko Tex Standard 100

www.centexbel.be/eng
The world's leading eco-label for textiles.

Pesticides Action Network

www.pan-uk.org
Independent site with excellent search to papers and information on wide range of issues, generally grown products such as fabric, timber, etc.

Recycling Guide

www.recycling-guide.org.uk

[re]design

www.redesigndesign.org
Portal for cutting-edge 'designers who don't want to make landfill . . . passionate about sustainable design and believe design can be a catalyst for positive social and environmental change. . . . (re)design seeks out and promotes products that are genuinely "good" and "gorgeous".'

Rocky Mountain Institiute

www.rmi.org
'An independent, entrepreneurial, non-profit organization fostering the efficient and restorative use of resources.' World leading environmental research and advisory organisation; comprehensive clear advice on wide range of environmental actions; includes links to appropriate enterprises in the USA.

Soil Association

www.whyorganic.org
Not only food but products such as textiles and furniture made from grown products – mattresses, some wood, paints, etc.

United National Environmental Programme

www.unep.org
Offers clear and comprehensive fact sheets and graphic displays of latest information on the state of different world regions on a wide range of issues: weather, recycling, flooding, transport, snow in traditional ski areas and chemicals. Excellent general and detailed information an all sustainability and climate change issues

World Health Organisation

www.who.int

Information on health effects of many environmental issues through comprehensive searchable database.

World Wildlife Fund

www.wwf.org

Excellent information site – comprehensive down-to-earth guide on all important sustainable issues. Carbon footprint calculator, energy and water saving tips.

SUPPLIERS

Ecomerchant

www.ecomerchant.co.uk

Natural insulation, building products, paints and rainwater collection.

Energy Development Co-operative

www.unlimited-power.com

Wind and solar power, equipment. Excellent links to renewable energy providers

Green Building Store

www.greenbuildingstore.co.uk

Natural insulation, building products, paints and rainwater collection. 'The Owl' energy monitor.

Green Heat Ltd

www.greenheat.uk.com

Independent Service Engineering (ISE)

www.iseappliances.co.uk

Very high quality long-lifespan washers and driers.

Interface Carpets

www.interfaceflor.eu

Major international carpet manufacturer: website proclaims environmental credentials resume of production issues relevant to all manufacturing and sales enterprises. In particular the 'Seven Fronts' programme.

Milestone Eco Design

www.milestone.uk.net

Kitchen units from recycled products.

Natural Building Technologies (NBT)

www.natural-building.co.uk

Suppliers and factsheets mainly for construction materials but including paints, plasters, etc.

Pilkington

www.pilkington.com

Discusses the full range of glasses including thermal performance and solar protection.

Saint-Gobain Glass

http://uk.saint-gobain-glass.com

Smile Plastics Ltd

www.smile-plastics.co.uk

Board/sheet materials for furniture and fittings made from a range of many different throwaway products.

Sonae Industria

www.sonaeindustria.com

Produces boards using recycled materials – useful information on sustainable issues.

Sound Reduction Systems

www.soundreduction.co.uk

Exemplary site explaining issues of sound in the home Downloadable product information for wide range of materials for every noise problem.

Urbane Living

www.urbaneliving.co.uk

Sustainable interior finishes, natural flooring, including bamboo.

Worcester

www.worcester-bosch.co.uk

Boiler manufacturer

Ventrolla

www.ventrolla.co.uk

Sash window company

TRADE ASSOCIATIONS

British Wind Energy Association

www.bwea.com

Corgi

www.trustcorgi.com

Directory of registered boiler installers and good safety advice about gas.

Energy Efficient Windows

www.energy-efficient-windows.com

Advisory and information site with full descriptions of many relevant topics and links to manufacturers of energy efficient windows.

Glass and Glazing Federation

www.ggf.co.uk

A trade association for all those who make, supply or fit flat glass, such as windows, film or plastics. This site supplies information about the Federation and glass and glazing to the general public. Useful information links.

Ground Source Heat Pump Association

www.nef.org.uk/gshp

Market Transformation Programme

www.mtprog.com/ApprovedBriefingNotes
Clear and comprehensive explanation of
different types of energy efficient
windows showing different construction,
glass and frame types.

National Energy Foundation

www.greenenergy.org.uk
List of installers and members.

Natural Gas Boilers

www.boilers.org.uk
Excellent independent site with efficiency
ratings of all gas boilers available in UK,
fuel cost estimator, method for boiler
sizing and other information.

Solar Trade Association

www.greenergy.org.uk
Explanations about solar energy and list of
installers by region.

INDEX

BIBLIOGRAPHY

Books

Alexander, C., *The Production of Houses*, OUP, Oxford, 1985

Alexander, C., *A Timeless Way of Building*, OUP, Oxford, 1979

Anik, D., Boonstra, C., and Mak, J., *Handbook of Sustainable Building*, James & James (Science Publishers), London, 1998

Ashton, John and Laura, Ron, *The Perils of Progress*, ZED Books, London, 1999

Berge, B., *Ecology of Building Materials*, Architectural Press, Oxford, 2000

Borer, P., and Harris, C., *The Whole House Book*, CAT, Powys, 1998 (Probably the most comprehensive and accessible book on ecological building)

Carson, R., *Silent Spring*, Penguin Books, London, 1999

Clifton-Taylor, A., *The Pattern of English Building*, Faber & Faber, London, 1987

Cofaigh, E.O., Olley, J.A., and Lewis, J.O., *The Climatic Dwelling*, James & James (Science Publishers), London, 1998

Harte, J., et al. Toxics A-Z – *A Guide to Everyday Pollution Hazards*, University of California Press, Los Angeles, 1991

Hawken, P., Lovins, A.B., and Lovins, L.H., *Natural Capitalism*, Earthscan Publications, London, 1999

Hill, Marquita K., *Understanding Environmental Pollution*, Cambridge University Press, 1997

London Hazard Centre, *Sick Building Syndrome*, London, 1993
Toxic Treatments – Wood Preservation, London, 1989
VDU Work The Hazard to Health, London, 1990

McNeill, John, *Something New Under The Sun*, Allen Lane The Penguin Press, London, 2000

Myers, D., and Stolton, S., *Organic Cotton*, Intermediate Technology Publications, London, 1999. (A telling book highlighting the developing world's dependence on the agro-chemical businesses in the developed world.)

Papanak, V., *The Green Imperative*, Thames & Hudson, London, 1995

Pearson, David, *The New Natural House Book*, Conran Octopus, London, 1998

Peters, V., *Stained Glass*, Crowood Press, Marlborough, 1999

Phillips, A., *Living with Electricity*, Powerwatch UK, Ely, 1994

Pilatowicz, G., *Eco Interiors*, J. Wiley & Sons, New York, 1995

Roaf, S., Fuentes, M., and Thomas, S., *Ecohouse Design Guide*, Architectural Press, London, 2001

Roaf, S., and Hancock, M., *Energy Efficient Building: A Design Guide*, Blackwell, 1992

Rousseau, D., and Wadley, J., *Healthy by Design*, Hartley & Hanks, USA, 1997

Seller, J., *Quiet Homes: A guide to good practice*, B.R.E, Watford, 1998

Vale, B. and Vale, R., *Green Architecture*, Thames and Hudson, London, 1991

Vale, B., Vale, R., and Perlin, J. *The New Autonomous House* Thames and Hudson, London, 2000

Van der Ryn, S., and Cowan, S., *Ecological Design*, Island Press, Washington, 1996

Weizsacker, E. von et al., *Factor Four – Doubling Wealth, Halving Resources*, Earthscan, London 1999

Wolverton, B.C., *Eco-Friendly House Plants*, Phoenix Illustrated, London, 1997

Woolley, T., and Kimmins, S., *Green Building Handbook Vol 2*, E & F Spon, London, 1997

Magazines

Building for the Future
Journal of the Association for Environment-Conscious Building
www.aecb.net/magazine

Environmental Building News
http://www.buildinggreen.com/products/allegory.html

Environment and Health News
86-88 Colston Street, Bristol BS1 5BB
Tel/fax: 0117 929 4342
www.ehn.clara.net, e-mail: ehn@clara.net

Green Futures
Magazine of Forum for the Future
E-mail: post@greenfutures.org
www.forumforthefuture.org.uk

ACKNOWLEDGMENTS

Author's acknowledgments

Many people have kindly read drafts and offered constructive criticism and corrections – all shortcomings remain mine alone. In particular I would like to thank Dan Davies of Solar Century, Nick Fordy of Berman Guedes Stretton Architects, Oxford, William and Gabby Lana of Greenfibres, Dr Kevin Lane of Oxford University Environmental Change Institute, Neil May of Natural Building Technologies, Dorothy Myers of Pesticide Action Network, Sue Roaf, Professor at Oxford Brookes University School of Architecture, Peter Tracey of TDP Environmental Engineers, and Christine Wordsworth. Ian Curtis, also of Oxford's Environmental Change Institute, gave valuable comments as well as much needed encouragement.

Many others provided help and information. I hope they will understand my gratitude even if I don't name them all. In particular, I would like to thank Colin Reedy of Metamorf Design, Bill Tippet of Milliken Carpets, Fritz Stroh-Wilde in Costa Rica, Dr H. Fischer of Auro Paints, Germany, Simon Garrod, Frank De Mita and Andy Allen. Hundreds of people readily shared information over the Internet, demonstrating the web's power to disseminate information and assistance. To all of them, wherever they may be, I extend warm thanks. Thanks to Sue Gladstone, Carey Smith and Frances Lincoln for their patience. Ruth Prentice handled the design calmly and skilfully under pressure, as well as ensuring a much needed flow of chocolate biscuits. The designation 'editor' doesn't do justice to Jinny Johnson's contribution: no author could dream of a more encouraging, calm and clear-thinking partner with whom to work. All at Berman Guedes Stretton Architects, particularly Roger Stretton, were unstinting in their support. At home, Alison, Philippa and Zoe as ever matched my obsession with their tolerance: lavish with support and encouragement, they made the enterprise possible.

Photographic acknowledgments

a–above, *b*–below, *c*–centre, *l*–left, *r*–right

Alan Berman 8*b*

Arcaid/Richard Bryant 1 & 153*r*, 106-107 (architects Gwathmey Siegel), 152-153 (architects GEA); Julie Phipps 7*b*; Alberto Piovano 47, Belle/Earl Carter 91 (design Alex Willcock/Don McQualter)

Auro Organic Paint Supplies 134*l*

Axiom/Joe Beynon 54*l*; Chris Bradley 16-17*al*; Dexter Hodges 5 & 120 (architect Carlos Ferrater); Jim Holmes 24*cl*, 33*b*; James Morris 20, 28, 29 (architect James Gorst), 81, 126, 141 (architects Ran Studios), 145, 158*a* (architect Claudio Silvestrin); Paul Quayle 32*l*

Barker Evans 57

Deni Bown 97*bl*, 97*bc*, 97*br*

Jon Broome/Architype 18-19, 89*a*, 96*b*, 174-175

© **Tim Coutts** 156*l*

DesignTex 31*ar* (William McDonough Collection), 149*l* (William McDonough Collection)

Christopher Drake © FLL 82

Edifice/Darley 6*b*; Dunnell 24*l*, 24*r*; Jackson 164*a*; Lewis 77*a*; Norman 7*ar*

© **Richard Glover** 14, 17*b* (architect John Pawson), 32-33*a*, 36-37*a*, 37*b* (architect Arthur Collins), 41 (designer Annie Gregson), 88-89*b* (architect John Pawson), 158*b* (architect Sophie Hicks), 165*a*, 165*b* (architect Sophie Hicks), 172-173

Polly Farquharson © FLL 64*l* (Kelmscott House)

Francisco Fernandez 54-55

Flow Gallery/Andy Keate 154*c* (designer Alison Crowther)

Freudenberg Building Systems 121*al* (Norament), 121*bl* (Noraplan stone)

Lars Hallen 84-85, 48-49*a*, 50*l*, 62-63, 69, 70-71, 73, 117*a*

The Interior Archive/Tim Beddow 75; Jacques Dirand 150; Ken Hayden 42 (designer J. Reed); Simon McBride 64-65 (artist Douglas Andrews); Eduardo Munoz 137*r* (designer Mary Foxa); Fritz von der Schulenburg 2, 65*r* (designer Jed Johnson), 98-99 (florist Barry Ferguson), 139 (designer Jed Johnson); Simon Upton 118 (designers Colefax & Fowler), 159 (designer Ilaria Miani)

Felicity Irons 117*b*

Ricardo Labougle 110*l*, 110*r*, 112*br*, 115*b*, 127, 128*l*, 128-129, 137*l*, 160, 166*b*

© **Frances Lincoln Limited** 166*a*

Lloyd Loom of Spalding 119*b*

© **Ray Main**/Mainstream 49*r*

Antonio Maniscalco 82-83

Matta/Loreta Bilinskaite-Burke 148

MetaMorf Design 154*r*, 169*b*

James Mortimer © FLL 168-9

Narratives/ Jan Baldwin 44-45, 163, 167

© **Mike Newton** 8*ar* (Vitra), 26*l*, 34-35, 104, 168*l* (Vitra), 169*ar* (Vitra)

Clive Nichols © FLL 111*br* (designer Sue Gernaey)

Paris Ceramics 112*ar*

Michael Paul 138

Red Cover/Winifried Heinze 38-39

© **Susan Roaf** 78*b*

Gary Rogers 6*ar*, 8*al*, 21, 22, 24*cr*, 25*a*, 56, 61, 67, 76, 78*a*, 79, 94-95, 96*a*, 97*ar*, 100-101, 103, 109, 116*a*, 125, 131, 149*r*, 164*b*, 170-171

Paul Ryan/International Interiors 13*a* (designers John Saladino & Sharon Casdin), 13*b* (architect Anna von Schewen), 23 (designer John Saladino), 26-27, 37*ar*, 44*l* (designer Jacqueline Morabito), 46 (designers Kastrup & Sjunnesson), 48*b* (designer Marcel Wolterinck), 77*b* (designer Christian Liaigre), 93 (designer John Saladino), 111*l* (designer Caroline Breet), 115*a* (designer Felix Bonnier), 133 (designers D&V Tsingaris), 155*a* (designers Haskins & Page), 155*b* (designer Christian Liaigre)

Sarie Visi/Ryno/Camera Press 134*r* (architect Johann Slee, production Ronelle Mayer), Sarie Visi/Lynette Monsson/Neville Lockhart/Camera Press 146

Smile Plastics Ltd. 171*r*

Fritz Stroh-Wilde 116*bl*

Studio eg. Inc 156-157

Trannon 154*l*

Simon Upton 6*al*

Veedon Fleece Ltd. 121*r*

VIEW/© Peter Cook 10-11, 25*b*, 52-53 (Jestico & Whiles), 68; © Chris Gascoigne 92 (architects Patel Taylor), 112*l*; © Dennis Gilbert 9 (Design Antenna), 17*ar* (Edward Cullinan Architects), 50-51 (AHMM); 58-59 (Child Graddon Lewis), 143 (architects Chance de Silva); Nick Hufton 43 (Peter Bernamont), 114 (Fraser Brown McKenna)

VK&C Partnership 31*al*

Elizabeth Whiting and Associates/Tim Street Porter 119*a*

Zen Flooring Direct 116*br*

Publisher's acknowledgments

Frances Lincoln Publishers would like to thank David Ashby for the illustrations on pp. 30–31, Andrew Melton and Hamish McMichael for the diagrams, Elizabeth Tatham for proofreading and Elizabeth Wiggans for preparing the index.

Editor: Jinny Johnson
Art Editor: Ruth Prentice
Picture Researcher: Sue Gladstone
Senior Commissioning Editor: Carey Smith
Editorial Assistant: Zoe Carroll